D0597220

Yugoslavia After Tito

Andrew Borowiec

Published in cooperation with the Carnegie
Endowment for International Peace

Yugoslavia After Tito

PRAEGER

PRAEGER SPECIAL STUDIES • PRAEGER SCIENTIFIC

Library of Congress Cataloging in Publication Data

Borowiec, Andrew.
Yugoslavia after Tito.

(Praeger special studies in international politics and government)
Bibliography: p.
Includes index.
1. Yugoslavia—Politics and government—1945-
2. Tito, Josip Broz, Pres. Yugoslavia, 1892-
I. Title
DR370.B59 320.9'497'02 77-83466
ISBN 0-03-040916-0

This study was written while the author was a senior associate of the International Fact-Finding Center of the Carnegie Endowment for International Peace. The views expressed, however, are the author's own.

Published in 1979 by Praeger Publishers
A Division of Holt, Rinehart and Winston/CBS, Inc.
383 Madison Avenue, New York, New York 10017 U.S.A.

9 038 98765432

Printed in the United States of America

For Juliet

INTRODUCTION

The purpose of this study is to demonstrate and analyze the pitfalls and difficulties lying ahead of Yugoslavia after the death of Josip Broz Tito. The author is convinced that in virtually every facet of what has become known as Titoism there is an inherent conflict potential. To ignore its existence would in many cases amount to accepting the false security of slogans and superficial assurances. The author is not predicting Yugoslavia's doom or imminent disintegration; he merely intends to point out that a powerful combination of adverse factors is piling up ahead of Yugoslavia's new leaders and, above all, its people.

In carrying out the research for the study, the author interviewed some 70 Yugoslavs and non-Yugoslavs in various capacities connected with the Yugoslav problem and its possible repercussions. They included embittered anti-Tito émigrés and confident party intellectuals in Yugoslavia; prosperous technocrats and disgruntled "guest workers" returning from the West; iconoclastic authors and officials barricaded behind slogans; Orthodox monks in Serbia and Catholic priests in Croatia; foreign diplomats and Western scholars at Yugoslav universities; members of workers' councils and students facing the problem of unemployment; journalists who have become masters in the art of self-censorship and political scientists who were surprisingly blunt about their concern for the future; Italian Communists alarmed at the prospect of losing a convenient Yugoslav "buffer zone" and Western analysts, whose predictions ranged from the proverbial "cautious optimism" to outright predictions of danger. A number of monographs, recently published books, and newspaper and magazine articles were also an important source.

In many cases, particularly when the delicate problem of who will succeed Tito was raised, the interviews in Yugoslavia were off the record. Those interviewed were perfectly willing to voice their fears and concerns as long as they remained anonymous. The author fully intends to honor this wish.

Conducting interviews was sometimes difficult because of the suspicious nature of Yugoslavia's present establishment. In addition, the National Security Law of 1974 limits all investigation of so-called sensitive subjects, dealing with the relationship between nationalities, between church and state, and, in fact, most forms of social research. Nevertheless, the author feels he has been able to evaluate the fears, hopes, and obstacles lying ahead in the murky post-Tito era.

It would be difficult to mention all those who helped in the preparation of the study. The author wishes to thank Charles William Maynes, formerly the Secretary of the Carnegie Endowment for International Peace. His critical comments were of great assistance to the author in developing his study, even though the author cannot assume that Mr. Maynes would share all of the final conclusions. The help of Slobodan Stankovic, a veteran analyst of Yugoslav affairs at Radio Free Europe's research center in Munich, was invaluable on providing statistical and background information.

CONTENTS

Yugoslavia After Tito

CHAPTER

1

EXIT TITO

> There are many people who do not wish us well. . . . We have many enemies even within our country, we have enemies who would even be capable of destroying everything that we have accomplished.
>
> Josip Broz Tito,
> Titograd, May 29, 1976

He has towered over Yugoslavia ever since it emerged from the bloodshed and shambles of World War II. Painstakingly and often ruthlessly, he has formed a vast and intricate party apparatus, directed the unification and reconstruction of the country, defended its independence, and provided the kind of leadership its survival required.

He has become a symbol of statesmanship and cunning and has projected many images in Yugoslavia and abroad: a tough, old partisan; a man who defied the Soviet Union against heavy odds; a benevolent father of his peoples; a world traveler in impeccably tailored suits; a dignified head of state in a shiny limousine; and a military leader in gold-braided uniform. Some have regarded him as just another dictator who covered his repressive methods with a smoke screen of slogans and jailed all those who challenged his rule or political doctrine. His personality cult has equaled that of the most prominent twentieth-century autocractic rulers, including Stalin and Mao Tse-tung.

To his confidants, friends, and many close associates, he is known as "stari"—the "old man." Indeed, on May 25, 1977, Joseph Broz Tito, the founder of modern Yugoslavia and its president for life, was 85 years old. It was also the 40th anniversary of his leadership of Yugoslavia's Communist Party, today the League of Communists of Yugoslavia (LCY). For the third time, the

Order of the People's Hero was bestowed upon him "in recognition of his extraordinary merits and his visionary and creative contribution to the historic victories of the peoples and nationalities of Yugoslavia." Congratulatory messages poured in from world leaders, Yugoslav sociopolitical organizations, and simple citizens. Still bright-eyed and alert, he toasted wellwishers at his walled residence in Belgrade's Dedinje residential suburb and in the evening watched a massive display by gymnasts at the Yugoslav People's Army stadium. Throughout the day, all Yugoslav radio stations transmitted accounts of the festivities, which ended with a display of fireworks. From countless loudspeakers throughout the multinational country came the lusty, chanted roar: "Tito is ours; we are Tito's!"

The watchword on that day, as on any other day in postwar Yugoslavia, was "Zivio Tito!"–"Long live Tito!"

It is simple biological fact that Tito cannot live very much longer–and in the time remaining to him, his grip on Yugoslavia is likely to diminish. There are notable precedents: in their last years, Spain's Francisco Franco and Portugal's Antonio de Oliveira Salazar presided over their country's destiny in name only. Tito's waning years have raised many questions and fears in Yugoslavia and abroad. To some they merely spell transitional difficulties during which Titoism will have to learn how to function without its founder. To others they presage the end of an era and the advent of mounting serious problems with equally serious consequences on the world scene.

On September 11, 1976, a terse Yugoslav government communiqué started alarm bells ringing around the world. Tito, it said, was suffering from "acute liver trouble," needed several weeks of rest and treatment, and was, consequently, canceling all scheduled appointments. Nevertheless, the aging marshal put up a brave front: he bade a cheerful farewell to a departing guest, President Nicolae Ceausescu of Romania, duly recorded by television cameras.

In the subsequent months, a flurry of newspaper articles, mainly in the Western countries, focused on the dangers and possibilities lying ahead for Yugoslavia. The concern was obvious: could that artificial country, held together largely by Tito's strong will and charisma, successfully weather internal and external pressures in its path? The internal pressures are represented by Yugoslavia's diversified national composition, exacerbated by the age-old disagreement between the Serbs and Croats, the two predominant national groups. The population explosion and the resulting demands of the rapidly increasing Albanian minority are also a serious problem. External pressures are invariably represented by the Soviet Union, which has tolerated Yugoslavia's political schism and nonalignment since 1948 but never really accepted it as more than a provisional solution.

The specter of possible Soviet intervention in a post-Tito Yugoslavia has preoccupied diplomats, politicians, journalists, and political analysts. It crept into the 1976 U.S. presidential campaign. The U.S. attitude, which is likely to set the example for the rest of the Western world, was typified in a statement by

Jimmy Carter. He said he would not go to war over Yugoslavia unless U.S. security was directly threatened. The subsequent winner of the presidential race added, "I don't believe that our security would be directly threatened if the Soviet Union went into Yugoslavia. I don't believe it will happen. I certainly hope it won't." Carter was expressing the view prevailing in the West that the Soviet Union would not risk destroying détente by armed intervention against a nation outside its own bloc. What Carter did not say is that Yugoslavia's drift closer to the Soviet Union may be carried out by peaceful means, largely beyond the control of the West and not representing a casus belli.

The announcement of Tito's illness coincided with another event which considerably damaged Yugoslavia's official image as a contented multinational experiment: the hijacking of commercial U.S. airliner by a group of Croat nationalists. It was a publicity operation; the leading U.S. newspapers were asked to publish a lengthy exposé of Croat grievances against Tito's Yugoslavia. Some complied. The publication further strained the difficult Yugoslav-U.S. relationship. But it helped to focus world attention on the Yugoslav national problem and its possible reverberations.

By mid-November 1976 Tito had recovered sufficiently to receive an important guest: Soviet Party Chairman Leonid Brezhnev. There were Slavic embraces and quips, jocular references to Western speculation about Soviet intentions toward Yugoslavia. The November meeting was hardly more than a facade covering a Soviet effort to shore up some of its shaky alliances in the face of two major unknown factors on the international scene: the advent of new leadership in both the People's Republic of China and the United States. The ideological differences between Yugoslavia and the Soviet Union remained basically unresolved.

No one denies that Tito is the sole founder of the Yugoslav brand of communism which is described, primarily in the West, as Titoism. The system has had no personal symbol other than Tito. Without this symbol Titoism may easily give way to instability, once again turning Yugoslavia into a vulnerable Balkan country, prone to internal splits and foreign subversion, bereft of leaders at home and trusted friends abroad. On the Old Partisan's eighty-fifth birthday, Titoism was still basically an evolving system. The links meant to hold the Yugoslav federation together have yet to be forged–if they ever can be. Yugoslavia has never been a "melting pot," but merely a grouping of nationalities with their divergencies, animosities, and quarrels. Despite some degree of cooperation–frequently considerable–local interests are paramount. The conflict between the quasi-pragmatic Titoist ideology and the basic devotion to the principles of Marxism has never been satisfactorily resolved. Tito himself has apparently been helpless in the face of this problem.

Titoism is many things to many people: workers' self-management or a gigantic waste of time on unproductive discussions; half totalitarianism and half democracy; a daring foreign policy of nonalignment which has antagonized both power blocs; a combination of Marxist slogans and Western market economy; a standard of living higher than that in any other Communist country but lower than that in the West; a policy of "free frontiers" and a considerable degree of freedom combined with the ruthless repression of anybody who challenges the old man and his system.* For years the system has vacillated, groping for a formula to combine Western efficiency with Marxist philosophy and to reconcile the feuding national groups which form the Yugoslav federation. While progress has been made in some fields, there are no easy answers to many crucial questions under the constraints of Titoism. At the time of Tito's death, Yugoslavia will still be half in the East and half in the West, with internal forces pulling the country in many directions. No amount of persuasion, repression, public rallies, and government edicts can change that.

While officially the succession has been clearly spelled out in the 1974 constitution formalizing the system of collective presidency, there are no ironclad guarantees that the system will work in the Yugoslav context. Pressures fueled by the possibility of power struggles, economic difficulties, precarious national relationships, and foreign intentions to influence Yugoslavia's post-Tito course are more than likely to be felt. Just how the Yugoslav edifice constructed by Tito will weather them is very much in question.

For some time, Western chanceries were inclined toward the comparatively optimistic and easy theory that despite the difficulties, "Yugoslavia will muddle through." Such an approach did not require alarm or contingency planning; it did not threaten alliances, priorities, or the balance of power in the heart of the Balkans. Recently, however, a more somber analysis of the Yugoslav question has begun to emerge.

On the whole, the U.S. State Department, the British Foreign Office, and most other Western governments would welcome the continuation of Titoism, including the predominant role of the Communist party, which is called the LCY, and despite the inevitable presence of the ubiquitous repressive apparatus.† The main reason for this attitude is the conviction that only the Communist party can keep Yugoslavia together and continue its nonaligned role in the world, including opposition to Moscow's domination. A nonaligned, politically independent Yugoslavia is very much needed in the kind of coexistence which has been maintained in Europe and the world under the policy known as détente.

---

*According to official statistics, East Germany has surpassed Yugoslavia's standard of living. When such factors as extensive Yugoslav trade with the West, availability of Western products and expertise, and free travel are taken into consideration, however, Yugoslavia's overall well-being is rated above that of the German Democratic Republic.

†According to Amnesty International, there are more political prisoners in Yugoslavia than in any other East European country.

A profound change in the Yugoslav internal system might lead to a major shift in the country's foreign orientation. The big questions are whether Yugoslavia's nonalignment will survive and whether the Soviet Union will have easier access to the Dalmatian coast naval facilities, so far extremely limited on Tito's direct orders. Conversely, should the new Yugoslav leadership adopt a tougher course against the Soviet Union, the whole concept of European security might be threatened.

The proponents of the muddle-through theory cite a number of factors to back up their comparative optimism. They argue that the main source of national friction, Serb hegemony, has been considerably diminished*; that the political parties that led to much prewar feuding have been eliminated; and that the warring churches have been stripped of their former power and their ability to influence political decisions. Yugoslavia may not be one nation, according to this school of thought, but in times of stress it has known how to "pull together." Its ambitious foreign policy has made a deep impact on much of the so-called Third World, thus contributing to a sense of pride at home. The federation's six republics (Serbia†, Croatia, Bosnia-Hercegovina, Macedonia, Slovenia, and Montenegro) have been economically interwoven and made interdependent. The steadily improving standard of living is a powerful unifying factor. The system, believers in the probable continuation of Titoism argue, can offer only a better future for all Yugoslavs; its disintegration would spell nothing but problems, whose magnitude few could escape.

The main argument in favor of the survival of Titoism after Tito, however, rests on the favorable international configuration. Détente has become strongly embedded, and neither of the superpowers seems willing to risk a return to a cold war era—or worse. Yugoslavia's neutrality and nonalignment are an important part of the global status quo. The country's considerable links with the West in the form of trade, Western tourism, and the policy of free frontiers for Yugoslav nationals might also be of some influence.

Among other factors, the more optimistic Western analysts cite the emergence of some degree of Yugoslav solidarity and the country's extensive defense preparations. Although it is highly doubtful that Yugoslavia alone could successfully challenge the Soviet Union on the battlefield, an outright Soviet invasion just might pull the Yugoslavs together long enough to trigger external reactions.

As long as Yugoslavia remains outside the Soviet bloc, the West does not seem to mind that in its foreign policy, Titoist nonalignment frequently includes

---

*Croat nationalists opposing Tito from their exile bases as well as a considerable number of Croats inside Yugoslavia challenge this view.

†Serbia includes the autonomous regions of Kosovo and Vojvodina.

strident attacks on "American imperialism." Although such attacks are annoying, in the final analysis they have not caused serious harm to the West. Some optimistically inclined Western analysts further believe that the Soviet Union will not risk upsetting the situation by openly interfering in order to bring Yugoslavia to heel when Tito is no longer alive. The gradual collapse of monolithic communism, illustrated by Moscow's repeated, although unwilling, recognition of "separate roads to socialism," is often regarded as further proof of the Soviet Union's limited leverage on the Yugoslav scene.

These unquestionably positive factors aside, it would be sheer naïveté to believe that the future of Yugoslavia will be free of disruptive processes of any sort. Whatever happens, one essential ingredient will be missing: the stability of continuing charismatic leadership of the kind only Tito has been able to provide. As a concept and as a system, Titoism depends on Tito perhaps to a greater extent than Stalinism depended on Stalin, although this comparison is perhaps unfair to a system which is immeasurably more benevolent than the reign of the late Soviet dictator. Tito's departure may well be followed by profound changes in Yugoslavia's present form of government, including drastic revisions of the concept of collective leadership, of the relations between the republics and the country's foreign policy. A quick look at recent history is enough to see the precedents: Nasserism did not survive Egypt's Gamal Abdel Nasser, and Gaullism in France is very much on the wane seven years after Charles de Gaulle left the Elysée Palace to die in the rustic solitude of Colombey-les-deux-Églises. Indonesia has lost its headline appeal without Sukarno's flamboyancy, and India after Nehru does not command the same international respect.

Even before Tito leaves the scene, the system he created is in the throes of contradiction and continuing soul-searching. The ostensible self-assurance of his planned successors, the platitudes showered by the regime on the country, mislead few. The apparent democracy of workers' self-management is undermined by party interference, apathy, inefficiency, lack of initiative, and corruption. Official nonalignment is more often than not mere camouflage for closely following the Moscow line in such wide-ranging areas as Angola, the Middle East, and Southeast Asia. The standard of living is rising, but the gap between the incomes of the richer and poorer republics is widening with it. The statistical Yugoslav lives better than ever before; at the same time, statistics can't measure his increasing frustration: contact with the West has convinced him that under a different system he could have done much better.

The country's future, the young generation, feels humiliated by the high unemployment which forces qualified university graduates to seek menial jobs in the West. The young are tired, above all, of slogans, the constant references to Marxism, the regimentation of endless party meetings, and the corruption of the technocrat class. While improving the standard of living, Titoism has also increased the expectations of the average Yugoslav. Although its repressive apparatus has to some extent defused the potential of internecine strife, its economic policies have exacerbated the differences between the republics.

Since the sweeping purges of Croat and Serb leadership in 1971 and 1972, Yugoslavia has had to face a number of extremely serious developments. They include the creation, in 1974, of an underground, "parallel" communist party, the Communist Party of Yugoslavia (known as the "Cominformist" party), generally believed to be directed from the Soviet Union, whose official aim is the restoration of orthodox communism in Yugoslavia. There is also considerable soul-searching over the concept of Yugoslav workers' self-management, with some indications that the economy might revert to a more classical communist model. Neighboring Albania's difficulties with its main backer, the People's Republic of China (PRC) have created the specter of that mountain country's possible return to the Soviet fold when the ailing Albanian leader, Enver Hoxha, is no longer in charge. The discovery in 1976 of a pro-Soviet conspiracy in Albania understandably heightened Yugoslav concern: should Albania move closer to Moscow, the leaders of any post-Tito regime would be under increased pressure.

The transition period will come at a time when national minorities throughout the world are demanding self-determination, or at least a bigger voice in shaping their future. They include Spain's Basques, the French-speaking Canadians in Quebec, the Bretons and Corsicans in France, and even the Jurassians in Switzerland. Nationalism is also rising in Scotland and Wales. These are serious factors to be considered by a country such as Yugoslavia, which consists of six major and 18 lesser national groupings.

It is clear that the men who inherit the leadership of Yugoslavia will be faced with hardly enviable problems and pressures. The main hope for reasonable success for these men lies in the comparative cohesion of the Yugoslav armed forces, which might have to be asked to step in as the ultimate guarantor of Yugoslav unity. A more encouraging factor, however, is the country's continuing existence as an economic entity since the end of World War II. The concept of "Yugoslav" federation has been established, and it has survived a number of crises, the most dramatic of which was the 1948 break with Moscow.

In politics, particularly Balkan politics, there are few guarantees and few certainties. Under the facade of official assurances and bravado which have accompanied Tito's last years, there is a considerable, gnawing fear of the future. Even the most optimistic analysts do not exclude the possibility of a major turmoil in the heart of the Balkans. The sound of the shot which in 1914 killed the Austrian Archduke Franz Ferdinand in Sarajevo and triggered World War I still reverberates around the world.

The country Tito will leave behind is a far cry from the wreck which emerged in the aftermath of World War II. The federation now has an area of 99,000 square miles (about two-thirds the size of California) and a population of 21.3 million. Its literacy rate is 85 percent, and its estimated per capita income, $1,180. The gross national product is $26 billion, and the average annual per capita growth rate, 5 percent. Macadam highways and railway lines now cut through mountain passes where Tito's rugged partisans fought and died. The scenic mountains are spanned by high-tension wires feeding power to industrial complexes which rise even in such distant and poor areas as Macedonia and Kosovo. The breathtaking Dalmatian coast offers a vista of modern hotel complexes, harbors crowded with pleasure boats, and the sturdy, cypress-shaded villas of the technocrat "new class." In Skopje, massive skyscrapers have risen from the ruins of a devastating earthquake. At the immaculate Zagreb airport, gleaming Mercedes taxis await foreign visitors. Satellite cities have mushroomed outside Belgrade, Zagreb, Ljubljana, and other major centers.

There is also the inevitable "other side" to Yugoslavia: shortages and corruption, mismanagement and waste, ethnic contempt, unemployment, frustration with the difficulties of daily life, and the threat of the omnipresent security apparatus, the watchdog of Titoism.

Foreign visitors to Yugoslavia–most of them in search of the sun and beauty of the Dalmatian coast–rarely notice the faults and injustices of the system. They seldom study the tensions simmering under the surface of comparative Yugoslav prosperity; they seldom enter into more than superficial contact with the inhabitants. Consequently, in much of the West, Yugoslavia is rarely thought of as an autocratic state beset by enormous problems and tensions. It was only recently that the country started attracting attention as a police state: much of the news from Yugoslavia during 1976 concerned the arrest and sentencing of dissidents, plotters, and outspoken intellectuals.* The situation has prompted the New York *Times* to say, "While Yugoslavia is sometimes viewed in the West as the least repressive European Communist country, the harsh reaction to dissidence is a reminder that Marshal Tito does not head a democracy, but a firmly Marxist one-party state."[1]

Milovan Djilas, once slated as Tito's heir apparent, demonstrated in his work *The New Class* the depth of bitterness of a disappointed Yugoslav Communist. To a large extent using his own country and his own leadership experience as a source for his sweeping conclusions, Djilas described Yugoslavia and other Communist nations as ruled by a new class of owners with complete monopoly of ownership. "This is a class," wrote the man who saw the ideals of his youth shattered,

> whose power over men is the most complete known to history. For this reason it is a class with very limited views, views which are false and unsafe. . . .
>
> Having achieved industrialization, the new class can now do nothing more than strengthen its brute force and pillage the people. It ceases to create. Its spiritual heritage is overtaken by darkness. . . .
>
> When the new class leaves the historical scene–and this must happen–there will be less sorrow over its passing than there was for

---

*According to Yugoslav authorities, in the 1975-76 period a total of 237 persons linked with 13 subversive organizations were arrested and jailed.

> any other class before it. Smothering everything except what suited its ego, it has condemned itself to failure and shameful ruin.[2]

One could argue with such conclusions, at least as far as Yugoslavia is concerned. On the whole, the system may have failed, but it could hardly be described as a "shameful ruin." But perhaps more than any other system it is full of imperfections—largely because of its fruitless search for a reconciliation between the two opposing political and economic doctrines in a multinational tangle subjected to what has been a one-party, one-man rule. Perhaps in another era, on another continent, the search would have had time on its side. Yugoslavia's vital strategic position between the Danube and the Adriatic, between the Balkans and the Alps, its multinational tangle, its inherent economic problems and overambitious foreign policy, clearly and simply spell danger. Tito has been able to contain this danger and, at times, even create the illusion of removing its specter. It is increasingly doubtful whether his heirs can succeed in carrying out such an overwhelming task.

Few of the men who hold leadership positions in present-day Yugoslavia have shown the qualifications needed to deal with the country's complex problems. Throughout most of their career, they have mainly carried out Tito's directives according to a strictly prescribed framework. Most of them are identified with their own national group and its problems rather than with the concept of a single nation transcending parochial quarrels and limited aspirations.

The Old Partisan has done as much as he could under the circumstances, given the limitations of his own doctrine, to lay the foundations for "Titoism without Tito." But he has not been able to overstep the ideological boundaries he himself imposed, for fear of shattering the edifice before it was completed. Above all, Tito has been hampered by his obsessive desire to demonstrate that, despite some degree of pragmatism and accommodation with Western concepts, Yugoslavia has remained a Communist state. It has been an extremely difficult role, and undoubtedly he will enter history as a man of stature. What he really needed was a different country, devoid of Yugoslavia's internal and external pressures, nationalist feuds, and the omnipresent concern with how to avoid antagonizing the Soviet Union.

NOTES

1. New York *Times,* October 3, 1976.
2. Milovan Djilas, *The New Class: An Analysis of the Communist System* (New York: Praeger, 1957), p. 69.

CHAPTER

2

THE SUCCESSORS

The bigger the head, the bigger the headache.

Serbian Proverb

Three men, all in their early thirties, posed for a photographer in the Bosnian town of Jajce in November 1943. The picture shows them standing close to one another in the coarse uniforms of Tito's partisans, squinting slightly in the autumn sun.

The occasion was the second session of the Anti-Facist Council of National Liberation of Yugoslavia (AVNOJ), generally regarded as the turning point in Tito's efforts to set the basis of his future control of Yugoslavia. Some historians consider it one of the most triumphant moments of the Old Partisan's career, "euphoric with a sense of achievement and impending success, . . . spiced with a feeling of successful defiance of the Germans."[1] The choice of the three for the official photograph was no coincidence: all of them were trusted associates who had stood by Tito in his most difficult moments during the antiroyalist conspiracy and anti-Nazi resistence, tough, ruthless, seemingly reliable, and devoted to their leader and the communist doctrine. All of them were successively designated as Tito's official heirs, and all but one were to fail him.

The men in the old photograph are Djilas, Aleksandar Ranković, and Edvard Kardelj. Since that 1943 meeting in the mountain town raided by German bombers throughout the gruelling war, their names have become part of Yugoslavia's modern history. To a great extent, their careers symbolize the nature of human relationships under a dictatorship which subjugates everything to the overall imperative of the continuation of the system. They are also a reminder that the designation of a successor in a Communist state can be a risky task.

Djilas was the first to be expelled from the party; jailed and eventually released, he lives in a fourth-story walk-up apartment in the heart of old Belgrade, at this writing deprived of his passport and the right to leave Yugoslavia. One of the most bitter critics of communism, he continues to publish his writings in the West. In Yugoslavia he is officially a nonperson, shunned by most of his former friends and associates.

Ranković, who attained the important post of interior minister, was fired in 1966 for overstepping the boundaries of his job: his men were tapping the telephone of Tito himself. He was also accused of opposing reforms. In a way, his case is less traumatic than that of Djilas: Ranković was merely stripped of his office but was not expelled from the party. All who know him claim he has remained loyal to the communist ideal, in a sense perhaps even stricter than the framework of Titoism. Tito, however, has torn up a written "testament" which formally designated Ranković his successor. Ranković continues to live in Belgrade, also a lonely man, frequently accused of pro-Soviet sympathies.

The third man in the photograph, Kardelj, a bespectacled, intellectual Slovene, is still around and continues to wield considerable power in Yugoslavia. He is 67 years old at this writing and is reportedly suffering from cancer. Although there is no formal word that Kardelj is to succeed Tito, most observers and Yugoslavs believe that if he survives the marshal, his will be the task of arbiter of the nationalist and ideological confusion likely to confront Yugoslavia.

The official successors are represented by a collective nine-man presidency, reduced from the original idea of a 23-man body by the 1974 constitution. The nine comprise representatives of each of the six republics and the two autonomous regions plus the head of the party, the LCY. The presidency has already started functioning in a vague way during Tito's lifetime, presumably to get the country accustomed to the system. The president of the collective presidency is to be rotated every year. It is generally thought, however, that one man in the group will wield more power regardless of who happens to be designated president during the annual rotation process. In the fall of 1976, the man thought most likely to supervise the process of transition was Kardelj, although some Yugoslavs believed that in the long run the role would fall to Stane Dolanc, also a Slovene, who has acquired comparative respect but little popularity as secretary of the Presidium of the Central Committee of the LCY. At this writing, Dolanc represents the party in the nine-man presidency, while Kardelj represents Slovenia.

To understand fully the problems confronting Tito and his associates in preparing the country for the post-Tito era, an analysis of the country's ideological problems and its constitution is in order. The overall aim is to secure the survival of Titoism after the death of its founder. This implies continuation of the three pillars of the system: workers' self-management, political nonalignment, and the federal organization of the state, based theoretically on the equal partnership of its component republics. Conscious of the problems that will face Yugoslavia after Tito's death, the country's top legal minds have worked for years to prepare a smooth transition, prevent possible conflicts, and keep Yugoslavia intact. The process, at least theoretically, ended with the adoption of the 1974 constitution–the third such document since the end of World War II. At this writing, the official view is that all questions have been answered and that Yugoslavia is ready to face the post-Tito era.

It is, obviously, an optimistic view. A careful analysis of the laws which are to govern the country's future, as well as the problems facing it, does not necessarily bear out this optimism. Under the facade of often strained confidence, a number of Yugoslav leaders have shown grave concern. The reason is that the combination of internal and external pressures on the country may be such that in the long run what is known as Titoism may have to give way to another political system. Given the Yugoslav leadership's long-standing commitment to Marxism, it is unlikely that it will incline toward a Western-style deomcracy. More likely, a more orthodox form of communism is in order, although such a transition is bound to cause considerable opposition. Already the regime has begun to brace itself for the post-Tito era by tightening up the security apparatus, curtailing freedom, and prosecuting all opponents in a vigorous manner.

The main problems confronting the future leadership and its ostensible desire to safeguard a Titoist Yugoslavia are (1) the Soviet Union's suspected intention to end the Yugoslav "heresy" and bring the country back into the fold, or at least reduce its freewheeling independence; (2) the fragility of the federal organization in which nationalist forces are very much at play and are capable of disrupting the federation; (3) the lack of tested, charismatic "Yugoslav" leaders, as opposed to men who have predominantly regional interests at heart; (4) the vulnerability of the country's economy, which vacillates between Western and Eastern concepts but is to a great extent dependent on the West and consequently prone to criticism by the more orthodox communist elements.

Since its liberation from Axis occupation in 1945, Yugoslavia has unquestionably lived in Tito's shadow. The marshal has not allowed the development of strong political personalities. His wartime companions and associates have carried out his directives and supervised the running of the state machinery, keeping most younger men out of positions of power or influence. Several political purges have depleted the pool of available talent. The approaching post-Tito era has led to a considerable tightening up of the internal regime, strengthening the hand of those who, for lack of better ideas, favor tougher control as the safer way of facing the future. Such an attitude is likely to undermine the much-needed popular support for Tito's heirs.

On the eve of the difficult transition period, Yugoslavia is facing the future with few qualified and respected leaders, a maze of multitiered and often overlapping institutions, and a complicated constitution consisting of 406 articles. The constant rewriting of the constitution shows dramatically that the country is basically groping for a lasting formula which will be hard to achieve in Yugoslav conditions without a strong personality at the top, backed by a widespread repressive apparatus. Tito, with his inborn toughness, shrewdness, and World War II aura, has succeeded in keeping the country together and defying external pressure. No laws and amendments can offer the same guarantees for the post-Tito era. It seems doubtful that the preponderant role of an individual–Tito–can be replaced by an institution such as the collective presidency.

The basic flaw in the system is the chronic tension it engenders, mainly because the government has been unable to determine how much freedom is safe. Any evolution toward liberalism is viewed as potentially destabilizing. Yugoslav party ideologues view national unity as the key to Yugoslavia's survival. For the time being, they have found no other formula for maintaining this unity except outright suppression of separatist tendencies and centrifugal forces–perhaps because no other formula is viable in Yugoslavia. According to Najdan Pasić, a leading Serb party theoretician, "We're conscious of the fact that internal divisions may provide an excuse for foreign intervention. Such divisions cannot be allowed and consequently will not be tolerated."[2] It is an explicit admission of how Tito's successors intend to deal with this problem.

Some analysts regard Tito himself as one of the last old hard-liners. By some, he is said to be more repressive by instinct, more heavy-handed, than most of his associates. In fact, according to this view, Tito has been acting as a drag on Yugoslavia's evolution toward a more liberal society. Extensive interviews in Yugoslavia do not bear out this view. The marshal's heirs appear much more insecure and uncertain of tomorrow. Rather than risk greater problems, they are inclined to keep the existing difficulties under the surface by fiat and repression. To what extent the Yugoslav public will tolerate repression without Tito's charisma is another matter.

There is a certain paradox in the attitude toward the post-Tito era: on the one hand, the longer Tito presides over Yugoslavia's destiny, the more time the country will have to try to reduce its internal tensions, solve its problems, and steel itself for the future. On the other hand, the longer Tito remains on the scene, the more stunning the shock of his disappearance will be, simply because all preparations for succession so far have affected only the inner sanctum and not the population at large.

The guarantor of Yugoslavia's and its Communist party's existence, surrounded by a domestic and international personality cult, Tito to some extent has blocked the search for a more pragmatic and democratic solution to Yugoslavia's problems. This, presumably, can be traced to his ideological communist background and his intimate knowledge of the explosive nature of Yugoslav national relationships. The longer the personality cult persists, however, the more difficult a transition to more normal conditions becomes. While it can be said that Tito has succeeded in projecting his country onto the international scene and keeping an independent, although frequently pro-Soviet, foreign policy, he has not achieved his goal at home.

When he leaves the scene, he will leave behind a nation basically in its political infancy, insecure, unconvinced by the quality of new leadership, and fearful of potential problems. Worst of all, post-Tito Yugoslavia will have no true allies capable of helping it out of its predicament in any concrete way. Its considerable stature among the nations of the Third World—a doubtful advantage at best—is not likely to help it in the event of external attack or economic difficulties. A sympathetic resolution at any Third World forum is hardly of any lasting consequence to a country in trouble. The unquestionable support of West European Communist parties for Yugoslavia cannot have any practical results. Trade with the West helps but does not offer a lasting solution. The most influential Western countries—the United States, Britain, France, and West Germany—have only limited leverage on the internal Yugoslav scene.

To understand what motivated Tito throughout most of his life, it should be remembered that he is the product of a tough, underground struggle against the prewar royalist government, a man whose political orientation was formed by Marxist literature and by years in the Comintern office in Moscow.* It is the kind of intellectual baggage that stays with one for life. Phyllis Auty, one of Tito's biographers, thus describes the marshal's Moscow indoctrination in the mid-1930s:

> He had mastered the communist rules. . . . He had learnt the formalized language necessary for all party writings and communications. These had to be expressed in certain phrases and words taken from current Soviet practice. . . . Constant repetition made them into clichés almost meaningless to the outsider, but the communist insider knew exactly what they meant. They had the force and message of a ritual. . . . Society was divided into "bourgeois oppressors" and "working masses.". . . The Soviet Union was "the protector of world peace." . . . Work within the party consisted of "correct" and "incorrect" lines. There were many phrases to describe the behaviour of those who followed "incorrect" lines, that is the independent, argumentative and disobedient people in the party: . . . these were "fractionalists," "adventurists," "deviationists," "opportunists," "reformists," "obstructionists against the leading party cadres." Yet the language, stilted as it was, conveyed real meaning, for it applied to real situations, the government was by any standards oppressive, antidemocratic and corrupt, and party members knew in general what they were fighting for, knew that they would not attain it without outside aid which could only come, it seemed, from the Soviet Union to whose help they owed their very existence.[3]

*Comintern, also known as the Third International, was founded in Moscow in 1919 to rally extreme left-wing parties outside the Soviet Union. It was dissolved in 1943, but some of its functions were taken over by the Coninform, created in 1947 and dissolved in 1956.

Even before Tito underwent his intensive Comintern training, the Soviet Union was his model. At his sentencing by the royalist Yugoslav court in 1928, the 26-year-old Broz (his legal name before he adopted the resistance pseudonym of Tito) exclaimed: "Long live the Communist International! Long live the Soviet Revolution." Had it not been for the Soviet Union's high-handed treatment of Yugoslavia after World War II, had it not been for Stalin's ruthlessness and Soviet efforts to interfere in Yugoslav affairs, it is doubtful that the break between Belgrade and Moscow would ever have taken place. As it was, Tito's energetic attempts to prove that he was not a heretic but very much a Communist weighted heavily on the Yugoslav scene: the biggest weakness of Titoism is that it is a system without a straightforward doctrine. It vacillates between communism and liberalism, between the straitjacket of party interference and the comparative freedom of the "socialist market economy." Tito's unquestionable popularity among his compatriots is mainly due to his defiance of the Soviet Union and his independent foreign policy. Few Yugoslavs go around boasting about the brilliant performance of workers' self-management: if anything, the system is accepted with resignation, at the same time fueling the seemingly inexhaustible supply of wry political jokes.

But while Tito could afford to vacillate without a challenge, at least at home, his successors can hardly remain in the same position. They are burdened with a concept which is anathema to orthodox Communists and inefficient and oppressive to non-Communists. It seems inevitable that a decisive change will have to take place at some stage.

It can be said with reasonable accuracy that there is no one in Tito's entourage or the party leadership who can command respect and confidence among the diversified mass of Yugoslavs. It is significant that frequently Tito is called "the first and last true Yugoslav." Kardelj, who is considered Tito's heir apparent, can also be regarded as a Yugoslav rather than a Slovenian leader. Dolanc has acquired comparative national respect but little popularity in his role as the party's "watchdog."

One can disregard the possibility of the political return of Tito's embittered old companion Djilas. Through his outspoken and sweeping criticism of communism, he himself has ruled out his participation in any kind of Communist regime. And it is highly doubtful that a non-Communist system could be installed in Yugoslavia in the foreseeable future.

The group of men forming Tito's ruling apparatus has not made an impact on the country as a whole. More frequently than not, they seem to represent, often stridently, the interests of various republics and regions. Such a situation can hardly have a unifying effect. All it can do is bring to the fore ancient rivalries, animosities, and parochial interests.

It took several years for Tito and his closest associates to elaborate the blueprint for succession. The inspiration came from neutralist Switzerland, an oasis of serenity in the turbulence of Europe. The Swiss model is extremely simple: a federal executive council or cabinet of seven men is elected for seven years. The presidency is rotated annually, and more often than not the Swiss are not sure just who is the head of the confederation at any given time. Switzerland does not belong to the United Nations but derives considerable profit from housing the United Nations' European headquarters and several score international organizations. It founded the International Red Cross, but its citizens, as shown in a recent poll, do not like to contribute to the developing nations. It has an admirable citizens' army, whose performance has never been tested in battle. Money from scores of nations is locked in the vaults of its discreet banks. It exports watches, precision instruments, light weapons, cheese, and incomparable chocolates. Its people are staid and generally unperturbed by events rocking the world. They do not believe in waste or ostentation: the president of the confederation does not have an official automobile for private use.

It is surprising that the Swiss model—at least its presidential system—inspired Yugoslav planners. Despite some similarity of mountain relief and the multilingual national composition, the two countries are very different. A system that may suit the placid Swiss is not necessarily likely to work in Balkan conditions, particularly in view of Yugoslavia's ambitions to lead the Third World in its quest for the "universality of nonalignment."* To transfer a presidential system which suits Switzerland to the heart of the Balkans shows a considerable degree of optimism—or naïveté.

The original idea of a collective presidency to replace Tito after his lifetime term differed considerably from the Swiss model: fully 23 men were slated to share this honor. The 1974 constitution, which incorporated 21 amendments adopted in 1971, trimmed the body to nine men elected for five years. Article 327 of the 1974 constitution further specifies that "the Presidency [of the Socialist Federal Republic of Yugoslavia] shall elect a President and a Vice-President from among its members for a term of one year according to a schedule laid down by the Presidency Rules of Procedure." Perhaps as an afterthought, the article added the following phrase: "The Presidency of the S.F.R.Y. shall announce and make public the election of the President and Vice-President. . . ." The Yugoslav population will thus be fully informed who its head of state is.

The president will be burdened with quite a few tasks, as specified in Article 328: he will represent the federation at home and abroad, convene and preside over the meetings of the collective presidency, sign acts adopted by the presidency and ensure their implementation, issue instruments of ratification of international treaties, and receive the credentials of foreign ambassadors and envoys. Moreover, he will be in charge of the armed forces and act as chairman of the Council of National Defense.

---

*The term is used frequently in official speeches and press articles to justify the official nonaligned policy.

Two major weaknesses of a rotating presidency in a country such as Yugoslavia are readily apparent. The first is that a constantly changing group of men will be faced with the task of imposing a one-party dictatorship on a multinational country. In addition to that, the impetus of Yugoslavia's ambitious foreign policy is likely to wane without the continuity of proven and known leadership.

In conversation with foreign researchers and diplomats, Yugoslav officials take great pains to stress that the system of collective presidency has become reasonably well entrenched and its members accustomed to its task. This assessment, according to all available but less official indications, is not quite true; although Tito does not intervene in every field of Yugoslav activity, he has reserved for himself during his lifetime several important domains. They include such sensitive fields as Soviet-Yugoslav relations, the nationality question, overall supervision of the security apparatus, and personnel policy. No one has ever contradicted the Old Partisan, who, for all practical purposes, rules supreme and unchallenged over Yugoslavia. So far, not a single man has emerged from the Yugoslav political spectrum capable of similar authority. Whether or not the intricate, involved, and cumbersome system of republican and federal assemblies, sociopolitical units, and self-management committees can function without a strong political personality at the top is constantly being debated with mixed feelings and considerable misgiving.

Tito, the president-for-life, is himself the architect of Yugoslavia's nonalignment and of its major international initiatives. He himself has made virtually every decision concerning Yugoslavia's relationship with the Soviet Union. In July 1976 he intervened in the fracas caused by the outspoken U.S. ambassador to Belgrade, Laurence H. Silberman, who criticized Yugoslavia's jailing of a U.S. citizen on charges of espionage. A precedent has been set by the old marshal: he, as the Yugoslav head of state, not only runs the country at home but projects its image abroad. It is reasonably obvious that if Yugoslavia is to maintain any semblance of impact on the foreign scene, particularly among the Third World nations, continuity of office is one of the prerequisites. The face of a new president every year will not do. It has done—admirably so—for Switzerland, which has no world ambitions and no impact other than in being the banker to the world, an occasional mediator, and the home of an impressive number of international organizations. But Titoism calls for an active—in fact a very active—foreign policy. Such an ambition will obviously be hampered by the lack of leadership continuity.

There is some talk among Yugoslav political scientists of the need to revise the rotating aspect of the system. Lubivoje Acimović of the Institute of International Politics and Economics in Belgrade believes that if the rotating presidency is maintained, it will be extremely difficult to preserve Yugoslavia's role in world affairs. To keep convincing the world—and particularly Europe—of the value of nonalignment, he said, the country has to have a well-known leader who has full authority without constant recourse to his partners in a collective presidency.[4]

At present such discussions center on making one member of the collective executive a primus inter pares—a first among equals. The main prerequisite would be that such a man be connected not with the interests of any single republic but with an all-Yugoslav concept. Since most leaders in present-day Yugoslavia are identified with their national group rather than with the country as a whole, many Yugoslavs feel that the choice logically falls on the president of the LCY. The party is an all-Yugoslav organization; it provides the doctrine and political guidance. Moreover, it is intimately linked with the Yugoslav People's Army (YPA)—like the LCY, an all-Yugoslav organization. At this stage 21 senior army officers are members of the highest party echelons. All Yugoslav general officers are party members, and party membership among lower officer ranks has reached nearly 100 percent. If the army is to be the ultimate guarantor of the country's unity and survival, its intimate cooperation with the party is essential.

The man who assumes the party's presidency will quite possibly become the natural arbiter of the collective presidency and Yugoslavia's official leader abroad. He must have the army solidly behind him, must have the support of the Serbs—the dominant national group—and at the same time must be acceptable to the Croats, the second largest Yugoslav nationality. Preferably, he should have a record of World War II resistance or "revolutionary" activity in the initial postwar period.

Kardelj seems to fit all the requirements. After Tito's death, he is the man considered most likely to become the party's president. Assuming that his health will allow him to steer Yugoslavia during the crucial transition period, he will have to move fast to prevent any disruptive forces from setting in. Tito himself is said to have told him that, above all, he must prevent the creation of a vacuum which might lead to prolonged uncertainty and power struggles.[5] As a Slovene, Kardelj is basically outside the main nationalist feud, that between the Serbs and Croats. An excellent theoretician of Yugoslav communism, he is generally regarded as one of the creators of modern Yugoslavia. Of all the leaders of present-day Yugoslavia, he is closest to Tito, having collaborated with him throughout the difficult years of antiroyalist conspiracy and World War II resistance. He is, as we noted, the only political survivor of the wartime triumvirate photographed in Jajce.

Like Tito, Kardelj was jailed and took part in prison courses on Marxism. When arrested, he was training to be a teacher. His subsequent role in forging the Titoist doctrine, with its special interpretation of Marxism, in a way fulfilled his longtime philosophic bent. Unquestionably, he towers over the men who are to become Tito's collective heirs. But he is not a demagogue, and his speech making is too intellectual to appeal to the masses. (This is a sharp contrast to Tito, who speaks down to the crowds, using frequent repetition and slogans.) It was Kardelj who expanded the Yugoslav theory of democratization through self-management, arguing that the system is superior to Soviet-style socialism and methods prevailing in China or the Western countries. Over the years, he has held government and party posts next in importance only to those of Tito.

But the contrast between the two men is not limited to their approach to speech making. Tito is easygoing and flamboyant, addicted to gold-braided uniforms and well-tailored suits, expensively furnished residences, and all the trappings of wealth of which he was deprived for so many years before reaching the summit of Yugoslav power. Kardelj is an introvert, a thinker who likes to take lonely walks in the countryside. He is said to be an international expert on mushrooms, plays the violin, and enjoys classical music. He is courteous in contacts with his subordinates.

As Tito's potential successor, Kardelj is likely to encounter considerable hostility from Moscow–but then, there are no known members of the Yugoslav inner sanctum who would be totally acceptable to the Soviets. What angered the Soviets particularly was Kardelj's statement in his work *Socialism and War*, in which he said, "It is wrong to assume that just because a country is socialist, it is immune from the temptation of waging war."[6] Kardelj is also on record as criticizing the Soviet approach to socialism, which provoked violent attacks against him in the Soviet press.

In his written statements and treatises, Kardelj has discussed at length the complex problems of Yugoslav nationalities. His theories of national interdependence and the need for a system of checks and balances to prevent authoritarian central rule have been incorporated into the constitution.

Kardelj's statement before the Slovenian party's Central Committee on August 26, 1969 is significant:

> I do not see anything at all new and tragic in differences among the individual republics. These differences have existed in the past, and will continue to exist in the future. But the question is whether we Communists will make the decision in solving the differences that pertain to cardinal questions of development of a socialist and self-managing society, and whether we will surmount them through the democratic mechanism of the League of Communists of Yugoslavia and thus become capable of political action. Or whether allowing all republican parties, governments and other agencies to work on their own viewpoint as if they were infallible or had no responsibility to others responsible for the overall social system, we will disintegrate and make ourselves incapable of any action whatever.*

As frequently happens in Communist countries, the theories are difficult to apply; however, in the final analysis, despite Kardelj's learned and unquestionably valid arguments, the central government in Belgrade invariably has the last word on any national question.

---

*According to the text released after the meeting.

In the long run, a number of observers believe that Dolanc may emerge as the ultimate successor once the transition period is over. He is one of the youngest members of Tito's entourage, 34 years younger than the marshal. His supporters describe him as one of the most able representatives of the "younger generation." He has been very much in the ascendancy. His critics claim that he is no more than a typical "apparatchik" (organization man), mainly concerned with order, discipline, and with keeping the party in line—a task in which he has succeeded without doubt. But whether he is capable of a more involved and more important role has yet to be proved. He is hampered by his lack of national prestige and his comparatively insignificant wartime role. In a country where the ruling establishment was almost entirely forged during the partisan struggle, this is very important. Moreover, Dolanc has a speech defect, a stutter, which often provokes giggles in his audiences. In a system in which leadership is invariably associated with oratory, this could be a serious obstacle.

In the summer of 1976 in Belgrade, succession speculation also centered on other men who are likely to play a key role in the party, regardless of the official composition of the collective presidency.* One of them is 64-year-old Vladimir Bakarić, for many years one of Tito's most influential advisers. A Croat, Bakarić lost his Croatian power base by being instrumental in carrying out the purges which took place in that republic following the 1971 student riots. Still, Bakarić has not lost his reputation as a relative moderate.

Aleksandar Grlickov, a Macedonian, is also likely to be projected into the limelight following Tito's death. At 53, he is secretary of the party's executive committee responsible for relations with the Soviet Union. General Nikola Ljubičić, the defense minister, is likely to play a greater role, being the only Serb of any consequence left in the party apparatus after the 1972 Serbian purges, which depleted the Serbian leadership.

Djilas, the man originally slated to succeed, is doubtful about the whole succession plan. While speaking in generally flattering terms about both Dolanc and Kardelj, he said in a conversation with the author, "With Tito, they're both very good. But without Tito?" As far as the official blueprint for succession is concerned, Djilas told the author bluntly, "I don't see a new leader, I don't believe in the system of collective leadership." Tito's old associate and his first designated successor thus appears totally skeptical about both the emergence of a new national leader and the ability of a group of leaders to supervise the party apparatus.

---

*In 1976, the collective presidency, in addition to Tito, included Vidoje Žarković, Petar Stambolić, Edvard Kardelj, Vladimir Bakarić, Cvijetin Mijatović, Lazar Koliševski, Fadifl Hodža, and Stevan Doronjski.

Was this merely an expression of bitterness by a man who has had the traumatic experience of losing faith in the system he helped to create? Or was it a sincere doubt about the future of his country?

Djilas himself disclaims any leadership ambition. There is an obvious reason for such a state of abject resignation: he and the system have parted ways. Djilas still has respect for Tito and some of his lieutenants, but his political credo is that the system has failed. To associate Djilas with the post-Tito succession would imply political convulsions which the Yugoslav state could ill afford, for internal and external reasons.

Reading Djilas's recent works, one can hardly imagine him rejoining a system which he so vehemently and bitterly stigmatized as a "shameful ruin." Besides, assuming that Djilas were willing to compromise his so frequently voiced principles for the sake of power his former associates would hardly be likely to accept *him*. He has been an outcast in Yugoslavia for some 20 years.

Tito himself has acted with supreme confidence when the problem of his succession is mentioned. In fact, according to the official line, there is no problem whatsoever! In February 1976 the marshal confidently announced that "I can leave at any time and nothing will change." And he added, "Those who are wondering about the fate of Yugoslavia after Tito have not understood our social system or our political and philosophical orientation."

Tito's more recent speeches have emphasized this self-assured view. An analysis of his most recent speeches shows no new ideas, no convincing argument in favor of serene transition. Inaugurating the new Belgrade-Bar railroad line in May 1976, Tito went on record with such phrases as "those people who think that Yugoslavia will disintegrate after me or after anyone else are wrong" and "nobody can break up these strong ranks, as powerful as a sea."

In addition to the succession issue, another problem clouds the post-Tito horizon: if the collective presidency survives the initial period and Kardelj and Dolanc emerge as the leading personalities, a heightening of national tensions is not unlikely. Despite their "all-Yugoslav" outlook and their apparent acceptability to the two major national groups (Serbs and Croats), the two Slovenes are bound to come up periodically against the pressures generated by Yugoslavia's complicated national relationship. Serbs, the biggest national group in the federation, will thus have to bow before representatives of one of the smallest republics. There is also the problem of the scarcity of men of stature among the present Serbian leadership. One is likely to find more able and forceful leaders in smaller Croatia than in Serbia, the nation which sacrificed most for the sake of a multinational Yugoslavia and which feels that it should have a lot to say about the federation's future. Croatia, with a higher standard of education, has never suffered from a paucity of political and business cadres. Whatever talent existed in Serbia was heavily depleted during the war years. The situation in itself can contain the seeds of internal conflict. And the last thing a post-Tito Yugoslavia can afford is personality rifts and a struggle for power.

The obvious conclusion is that the paucity of nationally recognized leaders and the possibility of internal conflict automatically strengthen the hand of those who believe that only a tougher internal system can guarantee Yugoslavia's survival. If this theory prevails, Yugoslavia is likely to turn more toward the "Romanian model" of strict, almost Stalinist, internal controls with some leeway in foreign policy matters. Such a system just might curtail the various disruptive forces within the country, reducing the possibility of its disintegrating or becoming an easy prey to foreign intervention. The price, in the form of less personal freedom, would be paid by all Yugoslav citizens.

This view, however, is not shared by all. For example, Bogdan Denitch, in 1976 assistant professor of sociology at Queens College and senior research associate at the Bureau of Applied Social Research at Columbia University, believes that firm foundations have been laid for a peaceful transition. According to Denitch, the proliferation of Yugoslav institutions and the many layers of authority may be cumbersome, but they give weight to stability. This assessment is based on the assumption that "everybody will have a stake in Yugoslavia's survival." Yet Denitch also feels that the current institutional setup is weak because it is continually affected by Tito's potential intervention. The politicians surrounding Tito constantly maneuver to foster their various aims, most often parochial in nature. If that is the case during the marshal's lifetime, one assumes that the trend can only increase after his death, except that there will be no person with Tito's forcefulness to keep nationalist tendencies in check–short of overall repression.

Of particular poignancy is the remark of a Western ambassador to Belgrade who, for obvious reasons, asked that his name not be quoted. During Tito's waning years, he said, "the hardest thing to figure out in Yugoslavia is the decision-making process." In short, too many people belonging to too many different organizations seem to be involved in often secondary decisions. Invariably, Tito's authority prevails on matters of consequence.

One thing is certain: The burden of trying to preserve Titoism without Tito will rest mainly on the LCY. The party, backed by the army, will be the main guarantor of Titoist continuity. Whether or not such a combination will survive the test of time is another matter.

Unlike the party in many other Communist countries, the LCY is a vast movement with membership open to all without many restrictions. Consequently, in addition to a number of sincere Titoists and believers in Yugoslav socialism, the party ranks have recently been swelled by thousands of simple opportunists. The tendency–never sanctioned by official decree–to require party membership for top managerial posts has understandably fostered enrollment. Thus, on January 1, 1976, the party announced the highest membership in its 57-year history: fully 1.3 million men and women. (By November the figure had increased by 100,000.) Significantly, 542,000 members fell into the category of white-collar workers. The working class itself, the blue-collar workers was represented by 366,000 members. (The remainder are agricultural workers.)

The party has a proud history of underground struggle and wartime resistance. Of the 12,000 prewar Communists, only 3,000 survived wartime guerrilla action, purges, and fratricidal strife. The major milestone in the party's irrevocable advance to power was the previously mentioned second congress of AVNOJ in November 1943. The council considered itself the supreme political authority of the resistance movement and, as such, consisted entirely of Tito's Communists. At that second congress in Jajce, where houses with tiled roofs perch over cascading waterfalls, the foundations for postwar Yugoslavia with its "Titoist philosophy" were laid. The resolutions adopted at Jajce pledged to establish a federal system with equality for all republics and included a number of other decisions incorporated in the subsequent constitutions.

Yet the search for Yugoslav equilibrium was not an easy one. The difficulties and ups and downs of the philosophy of postwar Yugoslavia are demonstrated by the frequency of new constitutions: after the first one in 1946, based on the Soviet pattern, a second one was adopted in 1963, to be followed by the last one in 1974. One reason for the almost obsessive preoccupation with the improvement of the constitution is the desire to prove that the Yugoslav system is better than the kind of communism advocated by Moscow. But the virtually constant writing and rewriting of the nation's basic law has led a number of political scientists to conclude that Yugoslavia under Tito has failed to build up a functioning system. There is only one other country which has had so many different constitutions in the same period: Haiti. And that nation's record can hardly be considered inspiring.

The organization of the party itself is reasonably simple and similar in its conception to those of other Communist states. At the top there is the 12-member executive committee of the Presidium of the Central Committee. The Presidium itself comprises 38 members, and the Central Committee, 165 members. Similar party organizations exist in the republics and autonomous regions. In all, Titoist Yugoslavia is a maze of assemblies, councils, other kinds of sociopolitical organizations, and other cells and units. Each holds numerous meetings and produces numerous resolutions, dutifully printed and submitted to higher authority. Most Yugoslavs interviewed by the author, however, did not feel that the proliferation of sociopolitical bodies had much impact on the functioning of the state. The various bodies are allowed a certain degree of criticism, limited mainly to mild imperfections. Like the press, these organizations cannot criticize the system itself or challenge any of its major precepts. In fact, any challenge to the role of the party, to the concept of self-management, or to the federal form of Yugoslav government is tantamount to subversion. Should a Yugoslav or a group of Yugoslavs have a better idea of how to run their country, they would be unable to make their proposal heard within the framework of Titoist Yugoslavia. For a country which stresses the democratic nature of its regime, it is a serious flaw and another potential source of future friction.

There is considerable discussion in Yugoslavia about the concept of Titoism, the country's specific form of socialism.* The discussion, needless to say, is mainly academic. A number of Yugoslavs feel that the continual accent on "socialism" tends to obscure other, more urgent problems which need solutions. The repressive nature of the regime stifles many ideas which could be generated by such an intellectually prolific nation as Yugoslavia.

The bane of the Yugoslav press is that there is no formal censorship: the authors—and frequently the editors—are responsible for the contents of their articles. Years of "living with the system" have taught Yugoslav writers and journalists to walk the proverbial tightrope cautiously—or risk jail. The result is that while the Yugoslav press is somewhat more adventurous and open than the press of the Soviet-bloc countries, it still offers its readers the usual fare of slogans, stereotyped "constructive" articles, and socialist boredom. The journalist is supposed to be "socially responsible" and is to stay clear of any "sensationalism." This definition covers a number of offenses.

According to Djilas:

> Intellectuals are forced into self-censorship by their status and the reality of social relations. Self-censorship is actually the main form of party ideological control in the Communist system. In the Middle Ages men first had to delve into the thought of the Church on their work; in the same manner, in Communist systems, it is necessary first to imagine what kind of performance is expected and, often, to ascertain the taste of the leaders.[7]

Such a system has created a class of comparatively affluent but frustrated journalists and intellectuals who give vent in endless coffeehouse discussions to their inability to write what they think. It should be stressed here that the system does not suppress free discussion provided it is limited to verbal exchanges in small groups and is not transcribed on paper. It is not so much a concession to democracy as sheer pragmatism: after all, the days when political clubs triggered revolutions ended with the unfortunate Paris Commune of 1871.

Officially sanctioned "discussion" within the party and other sociopolitical units is as stagnant and full of clichés as that in any Communist country. Perhaps one could trace this to Tito's early background as an ardent Communist, learning the vocabulary of the party in the drab offices of the Comintern of Moscow's Mahovaya Street. Still, since those days the marshal has traveled a great deal and has seen much of the world. His compatriots travel constantly, if not in search of work in the West, then for pleasure. But when they return home, they sit, straight-faced, through endless speeches which

---

*The word "Titoism" was coined in the West, but it is increasingly used in Yugoslavia itself in the Serbo-Croatian form "Titoizam."

convince few and amuse even fewer. Listening in at one typical party meeting, the author counted attacks against 42 different "isms" which apparently clashed with the Titoist view of socialism!

With the advent of Tito's heirs on the Yugoslav scene, the invariable question is whether the new leaders will allow the country's intellectuals any "safety valve." The author's feeling is that the tightening of the screw is very much in the offing. It is already reflected in the more strained contacts between Yugoslav intellectuals and members of foreign embassies. Again, there is no official edict: word is simply passed around, and the unofficial but omnipresent political barometer, which the citizens of all Communist countries know how to read, starts falling. Needless to say, the situation is highly changeable, and an improvement in the near future is not excluded. But in mid-1976, the foreign community in Belgrade was a frustrated group indeed, prompting a newly arrived Asian ambassador to exclaim that he found the Poles and even the Russians more open than the Yugoslavs. The diplomat felt that his dialogue with Yugoslav officials was limited to stereotyped phrases, rarely resulting in any meaningful exchange.

Another problem of the post-Tito transition which preoccupied diplomats in Belgrade in 1976 was the ability of marshal's heirs to deal with the Soviet Union. As mentioned earlier, Soviet-Yugoslav relations are the exclusive domain of Tito himself. It is Tito who decides how far Yugoslavia should go in placating Moscow and when is the time to put the Yugoslav foot down. Tito has not always been a perfect judge of the situation but on the whole he has succeeded in keeping his country out of trouble. Whenever the situation reached the brink, Tito knew how to pull away. A number of Western governments are seriously perturbed by the question of whether Tito's successors can show enough restraint in reacting to possible Soviet meddling. Conversely, a weak and quarreling leadership could be an easy prey to foreign pressures and maneuvers.

Tito himself has admitted on a number of occasions the existence of threats against Yugoslavia, both external and internal. Typically, he has not named them, but his audiences know exactly what he was talking about: the Soviet Union and the underground Communist (Cominformist) party. Time and again, he resorts to his favorite concept: "Who has given more for proletarian nationalism than Yugoslavia?"

As far as Yugoslavia's future is concerned, it is basically irrelevant who has done more for proletarian nationalism, whatever the term means to Yugoslav crowds. Tito has worked hard to secure a peaceful transition and an equally peaceful future for his country. Unfortunately, he has worked with frequently contradictory elements, and his cardinal mistake has been to keep from power men and women of the new generation. The partisans have done their share for Yugoslavia–and reaped their share of profits. By not allowing younger people to step forward and participate in the government as equals, to be groomed as his heirs, Tito has put the entire concept of Titoism in jeopardy.

As his hour approaches, his heirs resort to the old and tested method of repression. It is hardly encouraging for the future of Titoism.

A Yugoslav critic of the regime told the author that what perturbs him most is that the whole Titoist doctrine consists of a series of contradictions. Without Tito's dominating personality, he said, he felt these contradictions were more than likely to explode, shattering the edifice the Old Partisan has so painstakingly created.

NOTES

1. Phyllis Auty, *Tito: A Biography,* rev. ed. (Harmondsworth, England: Pelican, 1974), p. 270.
2. Pašić in an interview with the author, Belgrade, May 1976.
3. Auty, pp. 114-15.
4. Acimović in an interview with the author, Belgrade, May 1976.
5. This statement was attributed to Tito by a Western ambassador in Belgrade.
6. Edvard Kardelj, *Socialism and War* (Belgrade: Yugoslavija, 1960).
7. Djilas, op. cit., p. 141.

CHAPTER

3

IN SEARCH OF A NATION

The awakening of national consciousness has currently become a deep spiritual process, and the battle for freedom, which is a natural continuation of this process, has its basis in a fundamental moral principle and foundation.

From the "Declaration of the Headquarters of the Croatian National Liberation Forces"
September 11, 1976

The watchword is "bratsvo i jedinstvo"–brotherhood and unity. In virtually every major and minor city of the multinational federation, boulevards and streets are named with the slogan. It is hurled at mass rallies, roared by marching troops, repeated by tireless party organizers.

The task of forging one nation out of the 24 Yugoslav national groups has proved too overwhelming even for a man with Tito's drive and devotion to the concept of Yugoslav unity. The facts are outspoken enough: in the 1971 census, out of the total of 20,522,972 Yugoslav citizens, only 273,077 declared their nationality as "Yugoslav." The others described themselves as Serbs, Croats, Slovenes, Montenegrins, Albanians, and so on. In the end, Tito and his party had little choice: national particularism had to be allowed, but under the watchful eye of the federal government. The Croat demonstrations in the autumn of 1971 in favor of greater autonomy were the last example of pent-up nationalist feeling spilling into the streets. Since then, nationalist tendencies in Yugoslavia have been controlled and to some extent repressed. No one has a ready answer as to whether they can be contained to the same degree without Tito.

More and more Yugoslav leaders accept the fact that, regardless of the nature of the country's political system, Yugoslavia will always be faced with a virtually insoluble national identity problem. With the exception of the Albanian, Hungarian, and Romanian minorities, the citizens of Yugoslavia are Slavs. But being a Slav, even a southern Slav, does not necessarily offer a passport to unity. The problem gnawed at the shaky foundations of the Yugoslav kingdom between the two world wars. Since the Communist takeover, the dilemma has been increased by the fact that members of the ruling Communist party themselves seem to be devoted to nationalist concepts. More often than not, their priority is the republic and not the federation. Basically Yugoslavia has remained a tangle of "narodi" (peoples), whose roots are within Yugoslavia's present borders, and "narodnosti" (nationalities), whose origins lie outside Yugoslavia and who frequently have nothing in common with the concept of a homeland for "southern Slavs." Various official claims that the younger generation considers itself "Yugoslav" can be regarded as optimistic at best, as party propaganda at worst. The problem creates a serious conflict potential for the future.

As the Tito era draws to a close, any claim that there is one "Yugoslav" nation cannot be taken seriously. The very nature of the least homogeneous country in Europe spells problems. Having experimented with decentralization and then with stricter federal controls, the regime, uneasily, decided that the best course was to recognize a mild form of national regionalism rather than to repress it totally. The best hope for some form of Yugoslav unity lies in the interdependence of the six republics and two autonomous regions, the similarity of the semiindustrial civilization fostered by the Titoist system, and the proverbial "strength in unity."

It is often suggested that an external threat would provide the most effective unifying factor for Yugoslavia. To some extent this was proved after Tito's break with the Soviet Union. Yet the pressures at that time were mainly political and economic, confronting the leadership rather than the population at large. Yugoslavia has yet to show how it would "pull together" in the event of a real threat against the largely artificial entity originally mapped out by the treaties of Saint-Germain, Neuilly, and Trianon after World War I. What happened in the wake of the Nazi attack in 1941 is not particularly encouraging. Strong nationalist tendencies, from the prosperous Dalmatian coast of the Croats to the rolling hills and small villages of the Kosovo Albanians, are a slow-ticking bomb in the heart of the Balkans.

The record of the multinational federation is mixed. It began to fall apart shortly after it was formed in the wake of World War I; it was not able to withstand the onslaught and pressures of World War II. When it was put together again in 1945–after the loss of 1.7 million people, or 10 percent of the population, most as a result of fratricidal strife–Tito's charisma and his repressive apparatus mainly prevented its drifting apart. Once the Soviet threat caused by the 1948 rift subsided, the nationalist forces were at play again. Eventually the regime was forced to realize that "the former attachments to national cultures, traditions, and interests were not to be easily dissolved into the more abstract notion of higher-order, Yugoslav identity."[1] In short, Yugoslavia has remained a mosaic liable to fall apart if shaken too violently.

It is, basically, a nation of minorities. Even the Serbs, the dominant national group in the federation, represent only 39.7 percent of the country's total population of some 21 million. In recent years, there has been a trend toward a higher natural increase among smaller nationalities, particularly the Albanians, who represent over 7 percent of the population and who have no kinship with the Slavs or the concept of a Slavic state. (The Yugoslav Albanians have the highest birthrate in Europe, 35.3 per 1,000.) The income and standard of living discrepancies between the component republics have been increasing, causing an additional source of tension. For example, accepting the Yugoslav-wide per capita income as 100 in 1968, the republic of Slovenia had a relative per capita income of 183; Croatia, 125; Serbia, 100; Macedonia, 69; Montenegro, 64; and Bosnia-Hercegovina, 62. The predominantly Albanian Kosovo region in the Serbian republic had a per capita income equivalent to 33 percent of the all-Yugoslav index.[2] (However, the last officially available per capita income for Kosovo of $600 would make the percentage higher, considering that Slovenia's per capita income is generally quoted as $1,600.) While the wealthier regions, such as Croatia and Slovenia, complain about the need to support the poorer members of the federation, the underprivileged areas of Kosovo, Macedonia, and Montenegro clamor for more aid. It is a situation with no satisfactory solution in sight.

When Yugoslavia was born as a country after World War I, the initial euphoria was soon replaced by bitter disappointment. When the country faced the Axis invasion, it was dominated by Serbia. In a way, Serbian domination was one of the reasons for the swift collapse and disintegration of the state and the internecine fighting which ensued.

Tito's Communist party was perfectly aware of the inherent weakness of any Yugoslav national concept. At first, the party tried to solve the problem by stressing the ideological factor. National quarrels, party ideologues argued, were the result of the "bourgeois-capitalist mentality." When we come to power, they promised, national tensions will automatically disappear. This, clearly, was not the case. Nevertheless, the Communist party succeeded in drafting a federal system within which the republics and autonomous regions have an "equal voice" in running the state. Obviously, these equal voices can only be heard within the limited framework of the Titoist doctrine. The doctrine itself is sacrosanct.

It is apparent that the party, the administrative machine, and the defense and security apparatus have become infected with the omnipresent national question. While Tito's critics argued that the problem could not be solved on the basis of an artificial, multinational state ruled by a one-party dictatorship, the regime vacillated between solutions. Until 1965, the system was "unitary," with Belgrade firmly controlling the destinies of the federation. But this led to obvious tensions. Almost anything that went wrong was automatically blamed on "Belgrade" and, in Croatia particularly, on Serbian "imperialism." Consequently, the quest for national identification invariably became identified with criticism of the system. Factions and pressure groups within the party maneuvered to get the best advantage for their respective republics and clients.

Between 1965 and 1971, Tito switched to large-scale decentralization. The republics were allowed considerable leeway in economic planning, with Belgrade maintaining overall and often vague supervision. Needless to say, such matters as foreign affairs and defense were the prerogative of the federal government. But even there, minority groups and republics could voice objections and offer suggestions.

The fragility of the system was shown dramatically in 1971 with a university strike in Zagreb and loud Croat opposition to subsidies to the less developed republics. "Keep our foreign currency at home," chanted students as they paraded through the streets of Zagreb. The specter of civil war loomed over Yugoslavia. The mosaic seemed to be cracking. Tito himself thus justified the subsequent purges:

> If we had not gone into battle to prevent this, in six months' time there would perhaps have been shooting, a civil war. Do you know what this would have meant? Could I, as head of state and President of the Yugoslav Party, allow somebody else to come and establish peace and order for us? I have said that I would never allow this, that I would rather use the ultimate means, and you know what the ultimate means are.[3]

Indeed, Tito reacted forcefully, as he had promised. The "ultimate means" consisted of the largest purge in postwar Yugoslavia, with some 3,000 people ousted from their jobs. The purge affected the media, the judiciary, the youth and student federations, and the party and administrative apparatus. After Croatia came the turn of Serbia: Tito did not want to be accused of clamping down on the Croats alone. The party leadership in the two largest republics was, so to speak, purely and simply decapitated. No men or women of stature have yet taken its place. Yugoslav unity was preserved, but at the same time, the foundations for a peaceful post-Tito era were seriously shaken. Once again, the system reverted to more energetic central controls. True enough, limited national aspirations continued to be recognized. But the moment they took any form other than the propagation of language and cultural tradition, the government put its foot down.

The 1974 constitution spelled out in clear terms the nature of the Yugoslav federation. The republics "are states based on the sovereignty of the people and the power of and self-management by the working class. . . ." The autonomous regions are "autonomous, socialist, self-managing democratic sociopolitical communities. . . in which the working people, nations, and nationalities realize their sovereign rights."[4]

Despite the brotherhood-and-unity slogan and the federal constitution, whenever it comes to cash allocations, parochial interests come to the fore; brotherhood and unity are forgotten. Since 1971, Tito, son of a Croat father and a Slovenian mother, has handled the thorny national question himself. He alone has stood above the squabbles and feuds, a true Yugoslav. The big problem facing Yugoslavia is that there are no men and women capable of handling the national problem with the same authority and self-interest.

Recent world events do not offer much encouragement for the future of multinational concepts. Artificial powers, such as the Austro-Hungarian empire and the Ottoman empire, disintegrated long ago. In recent years, the tendency has been toward splits along ethnic and religious lines, creating particularly difficult problems for any leadership in a multinational country.

Yet on the whole, there are comparatively few voices in Yugoslavia in favor of the outright independence of various republics. There is a nationalist fringe in Croatia which claims that the area could stand on its own, as Denmark or Norway does. This fringe, particularly vocal in exile, points out that of the 33 European states, 16 have a smaller population than Croatia and 18 occupy a smaller geographical area. But anybody nurturing dreams of an independent or semiindependent Croatian republic must bear in mind that not all Croats live in the territory of the Croatian republic, that there is a large Serb minority in Croatia (14.2 percent), and that, although this republic provides a substantial amount of Yugoslavia's foreign currency income, it needs the other republics to prosper. A number of villages are mixed, and the population in the cities has been considerably integrated, mainly through marriages between Croats and other Yugoslav nationalities. In fact, with the exception of Slovenia in the north, there are no homogeneous republics. The various nationalities have been given "homelands," but they invariably share them with other minorities.

A number of Western analysts and diplomats feel that the complicated national makeup of Yugoslavia does not lend itself to splits. But to assume that would be to forget that whenever a country has split up in recent years, large-scale transfers of population have taken place. Surgery of this type is painful but not impossible. No one in Yugoslavia has suggested redrawing the existing frontiers between the republics: the government has gone as far as possible in this respect. And no one, at least at this time, is contemplating mass population transfers in Titoist Yugoslavia. After all, the system is supposed to have given the country "brotherhood and unity."

Perhaps the most recent small-scale example of population movement is the Mediterranean island of Cyprus. Before the 1974 Turkish invasion, the island's Greek majority generally demanded "enosis," or "union" with the 500-mile-distant Greek mainland. The Turkish minority (18 percent of the population of somewhat over 600,000) countered with demands for "taksim," or "partition." The Greek-Cypriot representatives argued that partition would involve impossible mass population transfers, uprooting over 200,000 people. Within a year of the invasion, the partition of Cyprus into two separate entities was a fait accompli: some 156,000 Greeks had fled or had been ousted from the Turkish-occupied northern portion, while close to 100,000 Turks were moved from the Greek south to the Turkish zone.

While by Cypriot standards the uprooting took dramatic proportions, it was insignificant compared to other population movements in the wake of World War II and other national upheavals. Eastern Europe itself offers such examples: when Poland's frontiers were arbitrarily moved westward, some 6 million Poles left the areas annexed by the Soviet Union. In turn, the Warsaw government expelled an estimated 8 million Germans from the Oder-Neisse territory, which was joined to Poland. The result was that, from a country in which an estimated 30 percent of the population were national minorities before World War II, Poland has been turned into one of the most homogeneous countries in Europe. But the operation caused massive national and personal trauma and considerable economic displacement. In Yugoslav conditions, any suggestion of large-scale population transfers would amount to a blueprint for civil war.

An argument frequently used in Yugoslavia to point out the country's viability is the economic interdependence of the republics and the advantages of unity. This argument is, indeed, convincing. Tito himself has used it on occasion, pointing out how much better off Yugoslavia is compared to most other "socialist" countries. "Are you going to throw it away?" is the key question in this line of reasoning. Indeed, not many Yugoslavs are willing to throw away the comparative achievements of the regime. But to assume that prosperity eliminates nationalism or breeds inertia in East European or Balkan conditions can be very misleading. The rival factions in Cyprus and Lebanon could only have gained by staying united, yet they drifted apart.

A clear distinction should be made between Yugoslav areas which have a vested economic interest in staying in the federation and those which feel that greater autonomy—or even independence—could be highly beneficial. There are, obviously, no separatist claims in Serbia, which originated the concept of a South-Slav federation, although at first for its own sake. Bosnia-Hercegovina and Montenegro are perfectly happy with the federation—and even to some extent with Serb hegemony. This is not exactly the case in the Macedonian republic, where pro-Bulgarian sympathies are still alive,* or the autonomous

---

*In a study entitled "The Macedonian Question and Bulgaria's Relations with Yugoslavia" (June 1975), Radio Free Europe analyst Robert R. King wrote: "Although the Yugoslavs do not provide any information on pro-Bulgarian feelings among the Macedonian population, it seems apparent that some such sentiment does exist. 'Nationalist deviations' (which would include Bulgarian consciousness, as well as other nationality problems) are consistently listed in the litany of difficulties the Macedonian party and government faces. Another very strong reflection of the Yugoslavs' concern in this regard is the vehemence

region of Kosovo, inhabited mainly by the Albanian minority. Prosperous Slovenia, with a population of less than 2 million, considers itself too small and too vulnerable to stand on its own. Besides, the pragmatic Slovenians realize that the federation is the best market for their products—as well as the supplier of some 20 percent of the republic's labor force.

The main problem, however, is posed by the Croatian republic, with a population of some 4.5 million, which controls approximately 50 percent of Yugoslavia's foreign trade and provides an estimated 70 percent of the country's foreign-currency income. It is generally considered that the age-old Serbo-Croat feud—dormant but periodically bubbling to the surface—is the biggest single threat to Yugoslavia's internal unity.

To understand the complicated relationship between these two largest Yugoslav national groups, a glance back is essential. The Serbo-Croat rivalry marred the existence of Yugoslavia between the two world wars. It exploded with internecine strife and mass murders during the World War II occupation—perhaps the most infamous page of recent Yugoslav history.

Yet the Catholic Croats and Orthodox Serbs have many things in common. One of them is language, referred to as Croatian when written in the Roman alphabet in Croatia and as Serbian when written in Cyrillic in Serbia. Allowing for some regional accent and expression differences, it is basically one language, frequently referred to as Serbo-Croatian.

Conquered by the Turks in the fourteenth century, after a series of uprisings against Ottoman rule, Serbia was granted autonomy within that empire in 1815. In 1878, it was recognized as an independent principality, becoming a kingdom four years later. The dream of "Greater Serbia" became a reality with the expansion of territory after the 1912 and 1913 Balkan wars. Serbia emerged from World War I as a victorious country on the side of the Western Allies and was the main inspiration for the Kingdom of the Serbs, Croats, and Slovenes, formed in 1918 and subsequently renamed Yugoslavia.

Croatia's independent statehood was ended in 1102 by a union with Hungary, under which Croatian nobles swore allegiance to the Hungarian kings. In 1527, Croatia's feudal barons turned for protection to the Hapsburg rulers, a suzerainty which was to last until the dissolution of the Austro-Hungarian empire after World War I. The period was marked by several rebellions, but on the whole, Croatia did not balk at its dependence on Vienna. Nevertheless, strong nationalist traditions have survived, bolstered by the nineteenth-century revolutionary movements and subsequently by the emergence of a new order in post-Versailles Europe.

During World War II, the occupying Axis powers established a puppet state of Croatia, headed by Ante Pavelić. During that period, an estimated 100,000

---

with which they attack Macedonians who have moved to Bulgaria and publicly announced themselves to be Bulgarians."

Serbs living in the territory of pro-Nazi Croatia were massacred, while thousands of others became the target of ruthless repression. The memories of massacres and persecution are still alive among the present generation of Yugoslav leaders. It is frequently said in Belgrade that there can be no solution to the problem of relationship between various Yugoslav nationalities without total eradication of the war's injustices, namely the wartime persecution of the Serb minority in Croatia. There have been no concrete suggestions from the Serbs of how to deal with the problem at this stage, and the generation of Croats born since the war resents the continuing reference to that comparatively brief period of Croatian history. Conversely, the predominantly Catholic Croats still point to the charred skeletons of churches where avenging Orthodox Serbs burned alive Croat men, women, and children. These are not the distant memories of the seventeenth-century Battle of the Boyne which haunt Ulster: these events took place only 35 years ago.

The Serbian charge of Croat "collaboration" with the Nazi powers may be justified in the context of the Yugoslav resistance movement, but not in terms of Croat history. Many Croats feel that their ties to the Yugoslav federation are the result of a quirk of history, that Croatia could equally well have joined Austria or even Italy. Thus, it was not surprising that Croat quisling Pavelić gained a widespread following or that the main targets of his Ustashi troopers were Serbs, the symbol of prewar domination.* The fact that many Croats also joined Tito's partisans in fighting for a unified Yugoslavia further showed the trauma of a major national group which has been groping for some form of national identity and recognition.

Perhaps the Croat claim to statehood is indeed based on flimsy foundations; after all, the last fully independent Croat state existed in the twelfth century. But the dream has never died, and as the area's prosperity has grown since World War II, the expressions of nationalism have become more and more evident.

Croatia's assets are many. They include the incomparable Dalmatian coast (the country's main tourist attraction), a high rate of literacy and education, and a modern infrastructure. Zagreb University boasts one of Europe's oldest medical schools. There are few squalid hovels in Croatia, where the cities bear the distinct imprint of Renaissance and Viennese architecture. Hard workers and good organizers, the Croats consider themselves a cut above other Yugoslavs. Many feel they have been unjustifiably victimized by being asked to

*For example, in 1939 Serbs occupied all posts in the office of the kingdom's prime minister, 89 percent in the ministry of the interior, and 96 percent in education. Of the 165 army generals in active service at the outbreak of the war, 161 were Serbs, 2 were Croats, and 2, Slovenes.

provide *their* money for the development of the other republics of the federation, with which they have little in common.*

Their bitterness has taken many forms, some of them quite alarming to the Serbs. When Croat claims for greater autonomy mounted in 1971, the republic's security apparatus reportedly prepared lists of Serb officials in the party and administrative machine. The Serbs once again felt vulnerable, prompting Tito's direct intervention. The subsequent purge included such respected Croat leaders as Savka Dabcevic-Kucar, president of the Central Committee of the League of Communists of Croatia; Pero Pirker, secretary of the league's executive committee; and Miko Tripalo, one of Croatia's two representatives on the Supreme Executive Bureau of the all-Yugoslav party.

It was significant that the people who staged mass protest demonstrations in the streets of Zagreb were not old partisans embittered by the disgrace of their leaders but students who, according to the official view, should consider themselves Yugoslavs and nothing but Yugoslavs. In December 1971 the 40,000 striking Zagreb students clamored for Croat, not Yugoslav, rights. To agree with the government that no nationalism exists among Croatia's youth only five years later would simply not be realistic.

The mass resignations, arrests, trials, and purges which followed only exacerbated the issue. A Serbian orchestra was pelted with tomatoes while playing in Zagreb in 1972; shouts of "Serbian swine" were heard periodically at the sight of visiting delegations from the neighboring republic. The wrath has subsided considerably since that time, but no farsighted Yugoslav leader dismisses the possibility of further turmoil.

"It is hard to say what the Croats really want." This statement by a senior U.S. State Department official is perhaps not as trite as it seems because, basically, the Croats are torn between the prospect of remaining the major financial backer of a Yugoslav federation—dominated, in their eyes, by Serbia—and the hazy vision of greater autonomy. The nature of Yugoslavia's internal political system does not allow much possibility of fully airing their grievances and finding appropriate solutions. The anger simmers on, and the best hope at this stage is that if ever Croatia finds itself on the brink, it will know how to pull back without irreparable damage.

There are few Croats today—apart from exiles—who in conversation with foreigners are willing to identify themselves as outright nationalists. Those who do, and who are willing to communicate with foreigners, see Serbia as the main obstacle to an equal Yugoslav partnership simply because "Serbia still wants Greater Serbia." To such Croat nationalists, the main Serbian driving force is imperialism. The expansion of the Serbian state which followed the 1912-13

*Slightly over 8 percent of Croatia's national income is deposited with the federal government to provide a fund for helping the less developed areas of Yugoslavia.

Balkan wars by the incorporation of Montenegro and Macedonia is proof of this "imperialism" to many Croats. Even today, in their eyes, Yugoslavia is a mere instrument of Serbian nationalism and empire building.

Yet the ideas of many Croats who voice bitterness against Serbs stop short of independence. Why? Simply because Croatia is not a homogeneous country. Of the republic's 4,426,221 inhabitants (according to 1971 Yugoslav figures), 79.4 percent are Croats. 14.2 percent are Serbs, and the rest, other nationalities of the federation. Having survived this long in the federation, Croatia–in the view of the nationalist fringe–is willing to continue, provided it has greater autonomy and control over its finances. If Serbia relinquishes some of its authority, then the federation can be saved.

The view is not unknown to the leaders in Belgrade, some of whom take it very seriously. Expressing the continuing soul-searching that goes on among the leadership, Acimović of Belgrade's Institute of International Politics and Economics agrees that the need to achieve "greater equality" among the republics is crucial. The problem is likely to be worse after Tito's death, and "a lot might have to be sacrificed in this field."

To convince the Serbs that they have to sacrifice anything at this stage might be a difficult if not impossible task, especially if their sacrifice is to favor the Croats, who have not yet "expiated" their World War II "sins."

On the whole, it seems that the quality of Croat leadership, despite the sweeping post-1971 purges, is much more impressive than that of any other republic, including Serbia. The Croat cultural organization with strong nationalist overtones, Matica Hrvatska, is immensely popular. It has attracted thousands of capable men and women seeking to give vent to the feelings they are otherwise unable to express. The author's talks with some members of the organization revealed that nationalism is a strong, vibrant force in Croatia and that its appeal is likely to be heightened in the absence of Tito's leadership and influence. There is a great deal of pure chauvinism among elder Croats, and many younger people have been influenced by it.

Not all Croats are satisfied with the reasonably tame expression of national tradition such as is allowed within the framework of Matica Hrvatska. If one were to categorize the varieties of Croat nationalism, three distinct forms come to mind:

1. dissidence within Yugoslavia against the imaginary or real domination by "Belgrade." More often than not today, this takes the form of passive resistance which could become disruptive in the long run or in an atmosphere of political crisis.

2. the right-wing émigré organizations, generally referred to as Ustasha, which frequently use terrorism as a weapon. They are anti-Tito, anti-Communist, and on the whole favor outright independence.

3. Soviet-sponsored provocateurs operating mainly among Croats working in West Germany. It is a fringe group whose obsession with Serb domination is exploited by the Soviet KGB.

It cannot be said that terrorism—Croat terrorism in this case—has so far amounted to a serious threat to the Yugoslav regime. This does not mean that the principal terrorist organization, Hrvatsko Revolucionarno Bratsvo (Croat Revolutionary Brotherhood), formed in Australia in the early 1960s, has been totally inactive. But its airplane hijackings and attacks against Yugoslav consular offices and other government property abroad have been hardly more than pinpricks. On the other hand, the Yugoslav security apparatus has not been inactive either: a number of exiles in Western Europe have been the victims of mysterious attacks. During 1976 alone, there were at least a dozen murders of Yugoslav exiles. They have included such well-known members of the wartime royalist forces as Uros Milicević and Mijobrac Bošković, both found murdered in a house in Brussels.

Yugoslavia has been making steady and often vigorous protests against countries harboring émigré organizations, particularly Australia, West Germany, Austria, Canada, and the United States. The September 10, 1976 hijacking of a Trans World Airlines plane by a group of Croats of the Croatian National Liberation Forces, which resulted in the publication, noted before, of a lengthy list of grievances against the Yugoslav government in such newspapers as the New York *Times* and the Washington *Post*, particularly angered Belgrade authorities. In the aftermath of the hijacking, a Yugoslav government spokesman issued a stinging attack against "influential and reactionary circles in the United States," charging they were allowed by Washington to "wreck friendly relations" between the two countries.

Such charges are not new. For years the Yugoslav government has complained that anti-Tito émigrés have not only been allowed but encouraged by the U.S. government to pursue their political activities. There are Yugoslav officials who believe that the United States is involved in a plot to undermine the Belgrade government, if not during Tito's lifetime, then when his successors take over. All denials by the State Department have had no effect on this point of view. The Yugoslavs are convinced that the well-organized network of Roman Catholic Croat churches in some areas of the United States is nothing but a cover for the Ustashi terrorists, condoned by the U.S. government.*

The extremist fringe of Croat nationalists could become much more dangerous in the event of serious ideological and economic problems in the federation as a whole. The economic difficulties that are likely to face Yugoslavia after Tito, particularly if mishandled by his successors, could easily give

---

*According to spokesmen for the émigré community, there are approximately 60,000 people of Croatian origin in the New York metropolitan area alone. Yet the 1970 census reported only 26,077 residents of Yugoslav stock—including Serbs, Slovenes, and other nationalities—in the entire state of New York.

Following the hijacking incident, various spokesmen for émigré organizations condemned the use of violence, at the same time stressing the existence of the "regime of terror" in Yugoslavia itself. This view was clearly reflected in the "declaration" issued by the Croatian National Liberation Forces in conjunction with the hijacking.

rise to serious disturbances in Croatia. The policy of "open frontiers," involving a comparatively large movement of foreign tourists and Yugoslav "guest workers" employed in the West, could also facilitate mass infiltrations of trained terrorists from abroad to exploit the popular discontent.* Escalation of violence, in that case, would merely be a question of time. The consequences might be totally unpredictable.

Longtime observers of the Croat scene do not exclude a dangerous movement "to the brink" by the Croats, particularly if the economic situation deteriorates. It must be remembered that the root of the nationalist demands of 1971 was predominantly economic. A new recession in the West would invariably reduce the number of predominantly Croat "Gastarbeiter," as well as the number of Western tourists flocking to the Dalmatian beaches. Unless the federal government is clever enough to lower Croatia's contribution to the federal "kitty" quickly and to a sizable degree, the brinkmanship may indeed get out of hand. There are no indications that the collective leadership would act with enough foresight in a time of national stress.

What perturbed the government most after the 1971 Croat disturbances was the obvious collusion that existed between Communist and non-Communist forces. When it came to voicing demands or protests, even members of the Communist party showed they were Croats first and, only later, Communists. With considerable alarm, the establishment realized that after 25 years of Titoism, a Croat Communist had more in common with a non-Communist Croat than with a Communist Serb. The events which rocked Croatia in 1971 exposed the fragility of the bonds which have kept the federation together. They showed that the population of Croatia is more Croat than Yugoslav. It was a significant revelation, and a more reflective regime would have drawn lessons from it long ago. Here again, the big question is the degree of the regime's leverage within the context of Titoism and the federal status it has created. As mentioned earlier, the party apparatus fears concessions toward the country's various nationalisms as potentially destabilizing. And no one in Yugoslavia under Tito's shadow can suggest that perhaps the whole nature of the republican and national relationship should be revised. Instead, under the leadership of Tito himself, the regime prefers to resort to purges, arrests, and repression. There are no visible signs that Tito's heirs will be more farsighted.

There is a view among some Yugoslav scholars that the resurgence of nationalism does not emanate from the people but that it is an "elitist" movement. That may well be true. According to Ranko Petković of Belgrade's *Review of International Affairs*, the nationalist problem is to a great extent increased by the party organization, which tends to exaggerate its importance. The first affected are various interest groups within the party. The population invariably

*The term "guest worker," from the German "Gastarbeiter," denotes migrant labor.

follows their lead. On the basis of this rationale, the rise of nationalism among the population at large and the resulting nationalist frustration seem to be built into the system.

In the mid-1970s, these frustrations made the average citizen of Yugoslavia prone, if not to outright nationalism, then at least to some of its forms. In addition to the criticism of economic inequalities mentioned above, there was considerable fear of the changing population ratio within the federation in favor of some of the smaller minorities to the detriment of the major ones. The two biggest national groups—Serbs and Croats—felt uneasy about the ultimate impact of the rapid population growth among the Macedonians and Albanians. Yet perhaps the biggest single factor fostering national frustration can be traced, ironically, to free travel outside Yugoslavia and free access to non-Yugoslav sources of information. As a result, the average Yugoslav perceives a clear discrepancy between what he feels he deserves from the system and what he is getting. The frustration is particularly acute among the workers returning from the West, men and women who have been exposed to a different economic and political system.

There are no official estimates, but it is believed that between 1952 and 1976 about 3 million Yugoslavs at some stage worked abroad, and many took their families with them for varying periods of time. This has created a high percentage of the population familiar with the ways and possibilities of Western capitalism. Their stay abroad has heightened their economic and political expectations. Their return to Yugoslavia has shown bluntly that some of their aspirations, such as social justice and real political power, can never be fully satisfied within the framework of Titoism. Frequently, these frustrated citizens turn to nationalism for succor.

In the case of Croatia, perhaps the most dramatic exposé of nationalist aspirations was made by Sime Djodan, an economist. When Djodan wrote, in several articles published in Yugoslavia prior to 1972, that the development of Croatia would compare favorably with that of Western Europe were it not for the area's "exploitation" by the federal system, he touched on a very sensitive nerve. The federation, Djodan claimed, blocked the development of Croatia and gave it nothing in exchange except the vague concept of "strength in numbers." The Croats, needless to say, seldom blame the difficulties on themselves. Traditionally, "Belgrade" has been and is more than likely to remain the bête noire.

Such complaints even led to the suggestion (only tentatively explored) that in order to avoid the stigma of continuing Serbian domination of the country, the federal capital should be moved to another "Brasilia" in one of the smaller republics. For a variety of reasons, including the cost of the project, the idea has never caught on. Yet many Yugoslavs still think that the transfer of the power center from Serbia might have a salutary effect.

The movement of population between the various regions and some degree of intermarriage have not appreciably altered the nationalist tendencies. It would take large-scale intermarriage and a new generation of children of "mixed" couples to affect Yugoslav thinking seriously. The apologetic remark by a Serbian guest worker returning from West Germany, "I married a Slovene–but she is a good woman," illustrates to some extent the degree of the problem.

While the Serbo-Croat feud is basically an internal Yugoslav problem, the question of the Kosovo autonomous region has both internal and external conflict potential. The Yugoslav Albanians, who live in Macedonia and Montenegro as well as Kosovo, were nearly 1.4 million strong and constituted some 7 percent of Yugoslavia's total population in 1976. (In 1961 there were 915,000, or 4.9 percent.) If the Yugoslav Albanians' high birthrate continues, they will become the third largest national group in Yugoslavia within four to five years.

To accommodate such a sizable minority, the Kosovo autonomous region was carved out in the Serbian republic. The reason that Kosovo did not simply become a separate republic is historical and emotional rather than practical. The last Serb battle against the Ottoman empire before the conquest of Serbia was fought on Kosovo Plain in 1389. The Serbs have always considered Kosovo part of Serbian heartland. Even today, despite the high and apparently still increasing Albanian birthrate, Serbs constitute 18.4 percent of Kosovo's population, which according to the latest figures stands at 1,244.000.

As the Serbs become increasingly outnumbered by the Albanians, intercommunal tensions and problems increase. While the Kosovo Albanians demand more autonomy from Serbia–and some fringe elements even talk about a linkup with nearby Albania–the Serbs are questioning the wisdom of further liberalization and concessions to the Kosovo Albanians.

The high birthrate, combined with the lowest literacy rate (50 percent) and the lowest per capita income ($600; the highest is Slovenia's $1,600) in the federation, makes Kosovo a major social, economic, and political problem for the Yugoslav government. Moreover, the Albanians are not Slavs and cannot be wooed as valid members of a South-Slav state. If anything, they are a restless minority, seething with frustrations and demanding a bigger slice of the federal pie. As their numbers grow, so does their national identity.

The federal policy toward Kosovo Albanians has been enlightened and quite conciliatory. Self-expression is not merely condoned but encouraged through daily and weekly newspapers and Albanian radio programs. The thriving Priština University has been growing steadily, offering courses in both Albanian and Serbo-Croatian, the main language of the federation. There has been considerable implantation of industry amid the rolling hills of the region. Priština, Kosovo's capital, rises almost like a mirage, with its jerry-built skyscrapers next to squat, low, old-fashioned houses lining unpaved streets. Manufacturing plants have been built in Priština, Peć, Kosovska Mitrovica, Prizren, and Uroševac. In 1975, half of the province's income was derived from industry. Still, Kosovo Albanians do not consider it satisfactory. By demanding more federal funds, they inadvertently touch one of the sorest points of interrepublican relations.

While, for most Yugoslavs, concern about the future centers on who will succeed Tito, Kosovo Albanians have an additional problem: who will replace Albania's ailing old-guard leader, Hoxha, and his equally ill and aging heir apparent and prime minister, Mehmet Shehu. There are a number of Kosovo Albanians who feel that without Tito and Hoxha on the scene, the time would be ripe for all Albanians to join forces. Needless to say, the Kosovo Albanians realize the advantages of the Yugoslav economic system compared to that of Albania. Yet some of them nurture dreams of influencing Albania's internal course in the years to come.

There are many Yugoslavs who feel that it would be politically expedient to simply get rid of Kosovo, thus reducing a serious point of tension and an equally serious drain on federal funds. However, the concept can hardly be brought to life as long as the myth of the "Serbian heartland" persists. Any territorial surgery allowing Kosovo to split away would have to be accompanied by a dramatic constitutional revision. Even public discussion of such a project would be highly explosive for Yugoslavia.

Contacts between Kosovo Albanians and the nearby republic of Albania are sporadic. There is an exchange program for artists, teachers and technical experts and formal cooperation between the University of Priština, with some 15,000 students, and that of Tirana in Albania. Every individual applying for travel to Albania is thoroughly screened, and a number are refused entry. The Albanian authorities prefer couples over 60 years of age to younger men and women, who are regarded as potential Yugoslav agents by that isolated mountain bastion.

Apart from the affinity of language, tradition, culture, and religion (most Kosovo Albanians are Muslim) with Albania, being a non-Slavic minority in a generally Slavic state plays a considerable role in the feeling among Kosovo Albanians that their position in Yugoslavia is precarious, particularly if Belgrade should ever fall into the Soviet orbit. This feeling of unease enhances small but nevertheless significant acts of nationalism. In 1975, scores of Priština University students were jailed for having organized a Kosovo national liberation movement demanding union with Albania. On February 7, 1976, a Priština court sentenced 19 Kosovo Albanians to hard-labor terms of from 4 to 15 years on charges of "Albanian irredentism" and "Stalinism."

This carrot-and-stick policy, so evident in Kosovo itself, underlines the weakness of the Yugoslav federal system. It heightens tensions, frustrations, and dissatisfaction. It spells problems for the struggling Yugoslav national hodge-podge.

The other autonomous region within the Serbian republic is Vojvodina. The Socialist Autonomous Province of Vojvodina, with a population of nearly 2 million according to the 1971 census, is Yugoslavia in microcosm. Ten national and ethnic groups are represented in Vojvodina, and five languages are officially used. Serbs make up 55.8 percent of Vojvodina's population; Hungarians, 4 percent; and Croats, 7.1 percent. Other nationalities include Slovaks, Romanians, Montenegrins, and Ruthenians. The reason for this diversity goes back to the time when the Austro-Hungarian emperors settled various national groups in the area to create a multinational bulwark against advances by the Ottoman Turks.

What makes Vojvodina unique in the Yugoslav setup today is its virtual lack of national tensions. The Serbs are happy because Vojvodina is part of the Serbian republic. The sizable Hungarian group (480,000 in 1971) has not publicly proclaimed desire to join Hungary. The Hungarians have few claims to greater autonomy and appear to be satisfied with the allowed degree of self-expression, symbolized by 195 elementary schools, a daily newspaper (*Magyar Szo*), and the Hungarian broadcasts by the Novi Sad (Vojvodina's capital) radio station. Some Hungarians have achieved positions of responsibility and influence within the party and state apparatus.

The situation in the Socialist Republic of Macedonia is of a different nature. Here the Yugoslav government has made a major effort to create a semblance of national trappings, mainly as a deterrent against Bulgarian claims to that portion of the federation.

Historically, Macedonia is a trapezoid area of land in the heart of the Balkans upon which Serbia, Bulgaria, and Greece converge and over which they have often clashed. What today is defined as Macedonia by the Yugoslavs has belonged to the Bulgarian empire, the Serbian Kingdom, and Greece. According to official Yugoslav figures, Macedonians numbered 1,195,000, or 5.8 percent of the population in 1971; in the Macedonian republic itself, the Macedonians represent a comparatively sizable bloc of 69.5 percent of the total population of 1,647,000. (Minority groups include Albanians, Turks, Serbs, and Romanians.) Macedonians also live in the neighborhing Yugoslav republics. Across the border in Greece, there are perhaps 200,000 people who could be described as of Macedonian origin, and the number of Macedonians in Bulgaria is estimated at 170,000. Neither Bulgaria nor Greece recognizes the Macedonians as a separate nationality.

For the Yugoslav government, the "Macedonian problem" is in some ways similar to that of Kosovo: it carries the germ of potential international complications, mainly with Bulgaria. Internally, the Yugoslav government has been laying heavy stress on developing distinct "Macedonian" characteristics. In fact, a major effort was undertaken to turn the local dialect into a Macedonian "language," and a government decree officially sanctioned a Macedonian alphabet and orthography. There has been a steady growth of the Cyril and Methodius University at Skopje, the republic's capital, and the number of schools of all levels has been appreciably increased.*

---

*The Cyril and Methodius University was the largest in Yugoslavia in 1976, with more than 27,000 students enrolled in 9 departments. In 1972, according to official figures, the republic had 1,360 elementary schools, 45 vocational schools, 36 secondary schools, and 42 schools described as for "industrial trainees."

After the disastrous Skopje earthquake in 1961, Belgrade staged a massive solidarity campaign in favor of the stricken city, again taxing the resources of other republics. Today, Skopje offers an impressive vista of high-rise buildings and broad boulevards, although crowded shacks and hovels persist on the city's outskirts. But despite this effort and the accompanying implantation of industry, Macedonia is still one of the poorer republics, and its inhabitants continually clamor for bigger injections of federal funds.

On the whole, it looks as if, under the federal Yugoslav system, Macedonian "particularism" has been satisfied to a considerable degree. Yet apparently some identification with Bulgaria persists, and it might be exploited as a disruptive element should the federal structure be put under strain.

Of no small importance in the Yugoslav national setup are the Muslims, more specifically Slavic Muslims, converted to Islam during the centuries of Turkish rule. They are regarded as a separate nationality rather than a religious group. In 1971, there were roughly 1.7 million Slavic Muslims in the federation, concentrated mainly in the republic of Bosnia-Hercegovina, where they constituted 40 percent of the population of 3.7 million. The main reason for the separate existence of that mountain republic was to find some form of modus vivendi for the three ethnic and religious groups inhabiting it (Muslims, Orthodox Serbs with 37.2 percent, and Catholic Croats with 20.6 percent).

On the whole, there is no "Muslim problem" as such in Yugoslavia. They are allowed complete religious freedom* and have shown no nationalist aspirations compared to those of some other minorities.

It is not the purpose of this study to analyze in detail the problems and aspirations of Yugoslavia's component national groups. The main objective of this chapter has been to demonstrate that the links between the various nationalities are generally artificial, subject to great stresses and prone to exploitation by pending conflict issues. Yet the federal system which has been operating under Titoism has, to some extent, created bonds between the various component republics and nationalities. Despite the unquestionable disparities, the existing bonds should not be dismissed as an important factor in favor of Yugoslavia's survival.

On the whole, however, despite some unquestionable good will and effort by many Yugoslavs regardless of their ethnic or religious background, Yugoslavia has never become a melting pot, as have nations based on mass immigration, mainly the United States, Canada, and Australia. If the model of these three countries were to apply, Serbian culture would have to prevail in Yugoslavia. In Balkan and especially Yugoslav conditions, this would be all but impossible, short of a dramatic suppression of local languages and traditions. The period between the world wars demonstrated that Serbia was incapable either of enlightened leadership or of a consistent effort to force assimilation. The obvious solution, if Yugoslavia were to survive as an entity, was a federal concept, roughly such as is being practiced today.

---

*Funds from oil-producing Arab States are funneled to Yugoslavia's Muslim community, helping, for example, in the construction of mosques.

But the system rests on fragile foundations. The problem is compounded by the rigid application of the basic principles of Titoism, which a priori rejects any view of national relations other than the one officially sanctioned. One cannot draw much encouragement for the future on the basis of Yugoslavia's recent history, much less on the basis of its more distant history. It is not impossible that the federation may be able to resolve the question of national relations within the context of some form of Titoism, even without Tito. But the national question is closely related to external problems, which do not always look encouraging.

NOTES

1. Gary K. Bertsch, "The Revival of Nationalism," *Problems of Communism*, November-December 1973, p. 3.

2. *Ekonomist*, Zagreb, 1969.

3. Tito in a widely reported speech on December 1, 1971, before the 21st session of the Presidium.

4. From Articles 3 and 4, Constitution of the Socialist Federal Republic of Yugoslavia.

CHAPTER

4

BROTHERLY INTENTIONS

Authors of such fairy tales try to present Yugoslavia as a helpless Little Red Riding Hood, whom the terrible and bloodthirsty wolf—the aggressive Soviet Union—is preparing to dismember and devour.

Leonid Brezhnev,
Belgrade, November 15, 1976

Early in April 1974 some 30 men gathered furtively in an inconspicuous private house in the Montenegrin seaport of Bar. The Adriatic lapped at the golden sands of the nearby beach. In the setting sun, the medieval center of the town was bathed in a purple hue.

The aim of the meeting was not to admire Bar's ancient beauty against the blue sea, but to approve a document brought from the Soviet Union by a secret envoy. The document, apparently drafted with the approval of the Soviet KGB, represented a blueprint for ending Tito's political "heresy" and reestablishing Soviet-style communism in Yugoslavia.

Luck was not on the side of the conspirators. Within two years, most of the participants in the Bar meeting were in jail, as were several hundred other persons accused of having espoused the Soviet Union's cause. Yet the Bar meeting added a concrete element to the specter of anti-Titoist conspiracy, which has haunted Yugoslav officials ever since Tito's break with Moscow. The clandestine Communist party of Yugoslavia—as distinguished from the ruling LCY—formally began its existence.

Almost exactly two years after the Bar meeting, on April 3, 1976, another significant but generally unreported event took place in the Dalmatian coastal resort of Dubrovnik. On that day, secret talks were held between a high-ranking

Soviet military delegation led by the chief of general staff, General Krilenko, and the top brass of Yugoslavia's army, navy, and air force. The talks preceded by four days the visit of the Soviet guided-missile cruiser "Feliks Dzerzhinsky," the destroyer "Reshityelny," and a submarine to the Yugoslav port of Split. There was no official comment in the wake of the Dubrovnik talks and the week-long Split visit. Some observers in Belgrade, however, regarded them as presaging increased Soviet interest in Yugoslavia in the approaching post-Tito era.

No one, least of all the Yugoslav leaders, has been able to fathom just how Moscow envisages dealing with the Yugoslav "rebels" once Tito, the most prestigious and determined rebel, is no longer on the scene. Although Western intelligence sources speculate about several Soviet contingency plans, ranging from outright invasion to a slow process of internal subversion, it is obvious that much will depend on the Soviet leadership which will replace that of Party Chairman Brezhnev.

The Yugoslavs, however, are aware of several important factors falling into two interlocking problems: Soviet interest in Yugoslavia itself and in the Balkan peninsula as a whole.

In regard to Yugoslavia, despite periodic assurances from Moscow, the Soviet Union is suspected of planning to establish unhindered naval facilities on the Adriatic coast; eliminate the Titoist heresy, which to some extent has contaminated other Communist parties in Eastern Europe; and foster a "friendly" attitude on the part of any future Yugoslav government. Last, but not least, the Soviets are suspected of wanting to punish the Yugoslav "culprit," the first country to break away from Soviet domination.

On the general Balkan scene, Soviet policy has been characterized by considerable efforts, heightened by the November 1976 visits by Brezhnev to Yugoslavia and Romania. Since World War II, the overall desire of the Soviet leadership has been to turn the Balkans into a kind of "cordon sanitaire" against the bogy of German revanchism or any expansionist designs by the Western powers. In 1957, the so-called Stoica plan was launched by the then subservient Romanian government with Soviet backing. Its aim was to bind the Balkan countries more closely together, thus weakening NATO's southern flank, protected on the peninsula by Greece and Turkey. The Stoica plan was a non-starter, as was a similar scheme put forward by Bulgaria in 1971. The Soviets soon realized that any initiative by their staunch Bulgarian ally was doomed to failure. Whether they have entirely given up their Balkan intentions is another matter.

It is generally believed in the West that the continuation of détente is of the utmost importance to the Soviet leadership and, consequently, that Moscow would be loath to embark on any drastic course of action likely to shatter the status quo in Europe. There are no indications, however, that the Kremlin has given up the policy of what some students of Soviet affairs describe as "creeping" communism, achieved through a slow, gradual process. Such a policy, particularly in relation to Yugoslavia, would be less likely to precipitate Western and particularly U.S. reaction.

The so-called Brezhnev era has been generally characterized by considerable stability in Soviet foreign and domestic policies. By the end of 1976, the 70-year-old party chairman had held the office for 12 years, twice as long as Lenin. Consequently, his leadership has had considerable impact on the Soviet Union, having covered one-fifth of the "Soviet experiment."[1] In general, the nature of Soviet leadership has always been stable: since the revolution, the Soviet Union has been led basically by four men, all devoted to the continuation of the same ideological line. What happens after Brezhnev is not so certain, however, and some Kremlinologists do not exclude the possibility of considerable changes in several areas, including the sphere of foreign policy.

On the whole, most Western analysts adhere to the view that Moscow's acceptance of Yugoslavia's independent stance has been provisional at best. Since World War II, the West has been unable to prevent the extension of Soviet influence in much of the Balkan peninsula, and this despite the wartime agreement between Churchill and Stalin setting the limits for such influence.*

The 1948 schism between Tito and Stalin resulted in a serious blow to Soviet expansion plans in the Balkans (in defiance of the Stalin-Churchill agreement): Tito closed Yugoslavia's frontier with Greece, thus cutting off all effective aid to the Greek Communist guerrillas. The Soviet press has often referred to Tito's action as the "stabbing in the back" of the Greek Communists, causing them to lose the civil war. It can safely be said that only Tito's stubborn personality, his international stature, and his skill in the art of brinkmanship have so far prevented the Soviet Union from asserting its will in Yugoslavia. And these factors are likely to be lacking dramatically once Tito no longer presides over Yugoslavia's destiny.

The Soviet Union's interest in controlling the Mediterranean has prompted Moscow to seek port and other naval facilities for its steadily growing Mediterranean fleet. The success of such démarchés has been mediocre, and the 70 or so warships of the Soviet Mediterranean fleet have had to rely mainly on anchorages rather than permanent facilities. The anchorages include one in the Aegean Sea off the Greek island of Limnos, one between Cyprus and the Syrian coast, and one near the Tunisian bay of Hammamet.

---

*The understanding was that pending the peace settlement, Soviet influence would be predominant in Bulgaria and Romania and British in Greece. In Yugoslavia and Hungary, the two countries were to share their role on a 50-50 basis. In Yugoslavia's case, according to Churchill's memoirs, the agreement was to set "the foundation of joint action and an agreed policy between the two Powers most closely involved, so as to favour the creation of a united Yugoslavia" (Winston S. Churchill, *The Second World War* [Boston: Houghton Mifflin, 1953], vol. 6, *Triumph and Tradegy*, p. 234).

The Yugoslav Adriatic coastline offers superior deep-water harbors, protected by strings of islands. Soviet strategists and admirals have been eyeing the coastline, and several efforts have been made to alter the existing law, which curtails the use of Yugoslav facilities by foreign warships. According to some East European diplomats, in the summer of 1976 the law was about to be drastically revised, thereby increasing the Soviet Union's use of the Bay of Kotor, not far from the Albanian border. It was Tito himself, according to the same sources, who shelved or even torpedoed the agreement, even though it was supposed to include a major Soviet grant to modernize the Yugoslav navy.

At present, the Soviet Union enjoys a refueling and repair facility in the Kotor Bay port of Tivat. A Yugoslav maritime defense law (a copy of which was made available to all naval attachés in Belgrade) specifies that no Soviet vessel can stay at Tivat longer than six months. There can be no more than two Soviet warships, not exceeding 4,000 tons (10,000 tons for auxilliary vessels), at any given time in any facility. (The phrase "any facility" would indicate that Tivat is not the only port used by the Soviet navy; but Western attachés have been unable to obtain a firm indication to that effect from the cautious and suspicious Yugoslav naval officials.) The warships remaining at Tivat must be manned by one-third of the strength of their normal crews. The warships must be disarmed and the ammunition placed under Yugoslav custody. All warships visiting other Yugoslav ports by prior agreement—and this includes those of other navies—can remain in Yugoslav waters for only seven days.

Western strategists, in general, regard an increase in Adriatic bases as crucial for the Soviet navy. Should the Soviets one day succeed in expanding their facilities on the Dalmatian coast, the impact on all Western planning in the Mediterranean area would be significant. The whole strategy of the already wobbly NATO southern flank would have to be revised. The U.S. Sixth Fleet in the Mediterranean, already dwarfed in sheer numbers of warships by the Soviets, would become even more vulnerable and exposed. New plans would have to be made for the defense of Italy, Turkey, and Greece. There would be a serious new problem concerning the possible diverting and transport of ground troops in the Mediterranean in the event of any localized or major conflict. In short, the Western military and strategic posture in the Mediterranean and southern Europe would become precarious.

That is why, as far as Western strategy in the Mediterranean and southern Europe is concerned, Yugoslavia is very much a key country. Although ideologically opposed to Western political and economic concepts and, in fact, a strong force in fighting these concepts at all available international forums, Yugoslavia is often regarded as part of the West's defense perimeter. Yugoslav leaders are keenly aware of their country's strategic importance. Consequently, quite a few of them are convinced that this critical geographic position, particularly as far as the West is concerned, gives them political carte blanche. In crude terms, this conviction is often translated into the freedom with which the Yugoslav state attacks Western and mainly U.S. international initiatives, convinced that the denial of bases to the Soviet Union automatically extends the protective U.S. umbrella over the Yugoslav territory.

In the summer of 1976, a railway link between the federal capital of Belgrade and the Adriatic port of Bar was opened. Domestically, the railway is bound to be an economic boon to Serbia and Montenegro, linking the land-locked Serbian republic with the portion of the Adriatic coast which belongs to Montenegro. The economic loser will be Croatia, which has most of the Adriatic coastline. But then again, few Serb or Montenegrin politicians are particularly concerned if the comparatively prosperous Croatian republic collects less revenue from transshipment of goods. The inauguration, however, posed another delicate question involving the future of Soviet-Yugoslav relations.

To some Yugoslav strategists, the Belgrade-Bar railway already looms as a potential Soviet Trojan horse, by means of which the Soviets could easily dispatch troops, disembarked in the Bay of Kotor, to the heart of the federation. It is debatable whether such an operation could be swift and efficient. Certainly, it would be easier than any move over the rugged mountain ranges which facilitated the partisans' operations in World War II and enabled them to tie down 32 Axis divisions at the height of an exhausting guerrilla war. Still, concern about the possible Soviet use of the Belgrade-Bar railway illustrates the kind of thinking which has preoccupied Yugoslav planners.

If one were to draw a graph illustrating the history of Soviet-Yugoslav relations since Tito's break with the Cominform in 1948, one would see sharp ups and equally sharp downs. Since the start of 1976, the graph has behaved in its usual erratic manner. This was the year of the arrest of a Soviet woman accused of spying in Zagreb, of several sharp diplomatic notes, and finally, of the East Berlin summit of Communist party chiefs, at which the Soviet Union had to bow to the increasing demands of nonsatellite Communist parties to pursue their own "roads to socialism."

There was also the trial and sentencing of Vlado Dapčević, a leading Communist political exile with close ties to Moscow, on charges of high treason. At the time of the Stalin-Tito feud, Dapčević had openly sided with the USSR and was jailed while trying to escape to Romania. While in exile after his release, he had apparently established close links with KGB chief Yuri Andropov. Andropov's name and Dapčević's intricate connection with Soviet activities in Yugoslavia are said to have figured in the court proceedings, held *in camera*. It is significant that Dapčević was arrested by Yugoslav authorities while on a visit to Romania and spirited across the border, presumably with Romanian complicities. As Dapčević is a naturalized Belgian citizen, the Soviet embassy kept a low profile during the trial.

Dapčević's death sentence was commuted to 20 years' imprisonment, but the significance of the event was not lost on anybody: it was a stiff warning to all Yugoslavs who might be tempted by the Soviet brand of communism.

Brezhnev's November visit to Belgrade somewhat attenuated the feeling of tension, although there has been no sign of any concrete result. In fact, almost immediately after the Soviet leader's visit, Tito and his aides reaffirmed that Yugoslavia would never join any "political, military or state community" despite "constant pressures being exerted on our country from various quarters."[2] At the same time, the official Yugoslav news agency, Tanjug, released a report which stressed that the Yugoslav armed forces were capable of fighting against "any agressor, whether by land, sea or air." The report, signed by the collective presidency on foreign and domestic policy, added, "Because of Yugoslavia's important geo-strategic position, and the ambitions of those forces to whom the fundamental characteristics of Yugoslavia's internal and external affairs are not acceptable, further pressures and attempts at interference may be expected."[3] There is no doubt that in the context of Soviet-Yugoslav relations, the timing of the report was significant.

According to Sergio Segre, the Italian Communist party's "foreign policy planner," Tito is reasonably confident that the world Communist movement has split up and that the Soviet Union's leverage possibilities have become limited, at least in the ideological sense. Segre, in a conversation with the author, claimed that the Yugoslav leader also seemed convinced of the limitations of the USSR's military role in the Balkans as late as the summer of 1975, when Segre visited Yugoslavia. The old marshal apparently assured the visiting Italian Communist delegation that "Soviet military intervention should be totally dismissed." He also claimed that "the Russians and Americans have agreed to keep Yugoslavia the way it is."

Was it wishful thinking, in keeping with Tito's own much-publicized policy of "hands off the Balkans"? There is no official record of any formal Soviet-U.S. agreement to effectively keep "hands off" Yugoslavia, although such a course would be beneficial, if not so much to the Soviet Union, at least to the West.

On the other hand, it has often been argued that the best medicine for the centrifugal national forces within Yugoslavia would be an external—namely Soviet—threat. It just might help to bury the petty parochial quarrels and unite the disparate national and religious groups against a country which, by now, many Yugoslavs regard as the only potential enemy.

It should be stressed here that the Russians and Yugoslavs have been consistently misreading each other's intentions and possibilities. After the 1948 break, Stalin boasted that he could get rid of Tito any time and at his convenience. Yet assassination and subversion plans failed, and Yugoslavia, amazingly, pulled together in that extremely difficult period. Neither is there concrete evidence that the Soviets have been assessing the recent Yugoslav situation objectively. If one believes East European Communist sources, reports by the Soviet embassy in Belgrade consistently stress tensions and dissatisfaction with Tito's workers' self-management, rarely mentioning the positive sides of Titoism.

Nor has Tito always been a good judge of Soviet intentions. In the summer of 1968, before Soviet tanks had moved into Czechoslovakia, the marshal insisted that Soviet military intervention could be excluded. For example, in a July 1968 interview with the Cairo daily *Al Ahram*, he was quoted as saying:

> I do not believe that in the Soviet Union there are people so short-sighted as to advocate force as a means of solving the internal problems of Czechoslovakia. . . . The situation in Czechoslovakia is not such as to endanger socialism there. If the West intervenes directly or applies strong pressures such as to endanger the social system, then Czechoslovakia has her army, her Communist party, her working class, to defend herself with.

The Yugoslavs' misreading of the Soviet behavior pattern can be traced to the near veneration of Soviet communism which characterized the partisan leaders during the war, despite the Soviets' late and inadequate help to the partisans, who had to rely on supplies shipped or parachuted in by the Western Allies. Such a dramatic disparity between Moscow's words and deeds for years failed to have much impact on the Yugoslav Communist leadership. But that, presumably, can be explained by their tradition of longtime ideological reliance on the Soviet model. Myths, among ideologues, are not shattered easily, particularly when they are created during years of underground resistance and the toil and blood of partisan combat. Only when, after the war, Stalin purposely attempted to denigrate the Yugoslav wartime record did Tito and his lieutenants begin to have some very bitter second thoughts. It took Djilas several trips to Moscow and much eye-opening before he realized the aim of Soviet realpolitik in the Balkans.

In the mid-1970s, the tendency in Western chanceries was, barring the unforeseen, to dismiss the possibility of a direct Soviet military thrust into Yugoslavia, mainly because of the considerable risks to Moscow. The elaborate structure of détente would collapse, and with it the obvious benefits for the Soviet Union, to mention trade as one example. What may happen, however—and this is much more serious in the long run—is a slow but determined effort by the Soviet Union to undermine the regime of Tito's successors. The available indications of Moscow's slow but steady subversive effort—the creation of the underground Communist party, the infiltration of the émigré organizations, and the exploitation of any dissatisfaction in the country—are significant straws in the wind. It is generally assumed that the Soviet Union wants any future Yugoslav regime to be unstable, the country to be plunged into political and economic turmoil, thus serving as a warning instead of a magnet to the Soviet Union's East European satellites. In such a setting, an "invitation" to the Soviet Union to "save socialism" in Yugoslavia would be an easy step. But many foreign observers feel that there will be no need for such an invitation: deprived of the strong, charismatic, and tested leadership of Tito and uncertain of Western support, Yugoslavia may eventually drift back into the Soviet orbit by itself.

It is conceivable that in order not to antagonize the West European Communist parties, generally insistent on Yugoslavia's "separate road," the Soviet Union is not harboring any intentions of turning the country into a full-fledged satellite. There has been speculation about Yugoslavia's becoming an "outer orbit" ally, which would be much more convenient to handle and yet would preserve an air of independence. Such a solution would also, to some extent, appease Western concern about the USSR's Balkan strategy.

Consequently, the much-talked-about possibility of a Soviet military invasion is more likely to turn into an "ideological invasion," which the country would be less likely to resist in the long run—and the outside world more likely to tolerate.

There are some Yugoslavs—Djilas is one of them—who believe that the Soviets do not object so much to Yugoslavia's economic system as to its policy of nonalignment and its resulting role among the countries of the Third World. The issue is not clear-cut. In many instances, the Yugoslav attitude coincides with that of the Soviet Union—on the question of the Arab-Israeli conflict and Cuban intervention in Angola, to name two recent cases. In fact, some Western observers describe Yugoslav nonalignment as a sham. But Yugoslavia offers no guarantee of always pursuing a policy close to that of Moscow. In fact, the suspicious Soviets fear that Tito would really like to create a strong "third force" that might, one day, clash with Soviet interests. It is thus more than conceivable that the Soviets will do all they can to make sure that Tito's successors have no such leverage and influence on the international scene.

To be sure, Tito's bold dream of turning his country into an independent, powerful force still persists. While Yugoslavs are prone to disagree about the advantages of a modified market economy versus those of a more orthodox model of socialist planning, few disagree with Tito's policy of nonalignment. Such a policy offers independence and prestige, a stream of African and Asian delegates seeking comfort and encouragement from Belgrade, an assured and listened-to place on the United Nations rostrum. While it puts no overwhelming moral obligations on its authors and executors, it creates a sense of national pride, thus adding another positive factor to the country's quest for internal unity. To some Yugoslav officials, the sympathy and backing of the nonaligned world represents an additional "insurance policy" against possible Soviet encroachment.

Thus, in assessing Moscow's possible reactions to the post-Tito regime, the likelihood of an armed putsch or military invasion should be dismissed—barring the emergence of new internal or external factors. What is more likely to happen is the intensification of a subversive effort that will try to exploit the national and economic difficulties, eventually bringing Yugoslavia back into the fold in one form or another.

There is, apparently, a Soviet plan for armed intervention in Yugoslavia. Its existence was disclosed in 1974 by a Czechoslovak defector, General Jan Sejna. Dubbed Polarka, the plan includes a classic pincer movement by Warsaw

Pact forces (Soviet, Czech, Hungarian, and Bulgarian) against Yugoslavia. Sejna claims the plan even calls for the violation of Austrian territory to reach the Ljubljana Gap, opening the road to the Adriatic. The movment of highly mobile armored columns would be accompanied by airborne landings in Belgrade, Zagreb, and possibly several other key cities. The operation would be aided inside Yugoslavia by terrorist acts of pro-Soviet Cominformist agents and even, it has been suggested, by Croat separatists. The latter, although basically anti-Communist, are said to be subsidized by the Soviet Union, incongruous as it may seem: any group willing to create turmoil in Yugoslavia helps Soviet interests.

It is generally believed that the Soviets maintain links with various Croat dissident groups within Yugoslavia and, particularly, in exile. Just how strong the Ustasha movement is, is subject to speculation. The myth of the Ustasha organization in such countries as Australia, West Germany, or the United States has grown to considerable proportions, with some Croats claiming that as many as 40,000 men and women are connected with the movement. More serious estimates have put the number of active Ustashi at less than 1,000. Still, they can boast a number of spectacular terrorist acts outside Yugoslavia, including hundreds of bomb attacks against Yugoslav offices, airplane hijackings, and political assassinations.

The aim of these extremists is a free Croat state, basically Catholic and anti-Communist. Yet, Western intelligence services do not exclude the possibility of some Soviet channeling of funds into a movement that may represent a strong disruptive force against a post-Tito Yugoslavia.

In 1970, one faction of the Ustasha organization, led by Branko Jelić, adopted a pro-Moscow line to the extent that it promised the Soviets a nonaligned "independent Croat state" that would grant the Soviet Union base facilities. Jelić later died in Berlin, and his movement all but disintegrated. But it was indicative of the possibility that Croat frustration may lead to the most bizarre overtures and alliances. The Soviet security service would not be doing its job if it did not try to exploit and infiltrate even the most obscure group whose aim is the destruction of Titoism.

Equally, the Soviets are believed to be actively promoting good will within the hierarchy of the Serbian Orthodox church, as well as stirring up latent pro-Bulgarian sympathies in the republic of Macedonia and Albanian unrest in the autonomous region of Kosovo.

The Soviet "national" strategy is simple enough: when the time is ripe, all the Soviet Union will have to demonstrate is that Tito's Yugoslav federation was basically built on the fictitious autonomy of its component regions. From then on, it would be comparatively easy to exploit and channel the potentially disruptive forces which feed upon real or imaginary grievances against postwar Yugoslavia.

The main arm of Soviet influence inside Yugoslavia, however, is old-guard Communists who have refused to accept Tito's brand of communism as a true expression of Marxism-Leninism. In the five years which followed Tito's break with Stalin in 1948, an estimated 80,000 persons were expelled from the Yugoslav party on charges of pro-Soviet orientation. (According to some sources, there were as many as 200,000.) These men and women constitute an important pool of Moscow's potential agents. They have been bolstered by disgruntled "apparatchiks" and technocrats ousted from their jobs during the purges and the general tightening up which followed the 1971 Croat distrubances.

It is generally believed that the Cominformist movement is directed from the Soviet Union, with branch offices in one or two other satellite countries. Among the best-known Cominformist exiles are Colonel Blažo Raspopović, the man reportedly in charge of training agents and saboteurs for work in Yugoslavia; Radonja Golubović, a former ambassador to Bucharest; Pero Popivoda, a partisan general of some renown; Mileta Perović, a former colonel in the Yugoslav army who describes himself as the underground party's secretary-general; and Bogdan Jovović, who until recently taught at Kiev University. Kiev, in the Ukraine, is believed to be the nerve center of anti-Titoist activity in the Soviet Union. All told, there are some 3,000 anti-Tito exiles in the Soviet Union, and most are believed to be connected with the Cominformist movement. Some are reported to be senior officers in the Red Army.*

The biggest single event which alerted the people of Yugoslavia to the Cominformist conspiracy occurred in September 1974, when 32 members of the illegal organization went on trial on charges of "associating for the purpose of opposing the people and the state to install a system contrary to self-management."

According to an official communiqué distributed by the Yugoslav news agency, Tanjug, the arrested were connected with "Informbureau émigrés"—the same organization which held the congress in Bar in April of that year. The accused men received sentences varying from two to fourteen years, but several lesser participants got away with one year of imprisonment only. By mid-1976, Yugoslav authorities claimed that about half of the suspected 200-odd members of the Cominformist party were under arrest.

The campaign against the Cominformists has continued with varying degrees of intensity. Some Yugoslav officials admit that perhaps the government has overreacted. And there are some foreign diplomats who claim that the "Cominformist scare" is mainly a smoke screen to cover up Yugoslavia's economic difficulties. Yet a careful analysis of the country's internal situation does not bear out his theory. It is obvious that as far as Tito and his followers are

---

*A number of Yugoslav officers and cadets in training in the Soviet Union at the time of Tito's 1948 break with Stalin are said to have refused to return to Yugoslavia. They have been integrated into the Red Army. In the past few years, however, increasing numbers of Yugoslav army officers have been undergoing training in the Soviet Union as part of Soviet-Yugoslav military cooperation.

concerned, any challenge to their ideological stand is potentially explosive. Also, the Cominformist Communist party could very well issue an "invitation" to the Soviet Union to "preserve socialism in Yugoslavia" should the internal situation become chaotic.

Significantly, the so-called Bar congress, at which statutory acts were adopted and a formal leadership set up, described itself as the "fifth congress of the party." In so doing, it attempted to nullify Tito's own fifth congress, which had approved his 1948 break with the Cominform, as well as the subsequent five congresses of the Yugoslav party, renamed the League of Communists of Yugoslavia in 1958. The congress was led by Komnen Jovović, described as a "retired man" from Peć in the Kosovo region, and Branislav Bošković, a professor at Priština University. Jovović reportedly obtained a blueprint for Cominformist activity while on a visit to the Soviet Union and was active in organizing cells patterned on those of the pre-World War II Communist underground organization.

The statutes of the underground party as well as its program took up fully 120 pages. Some of the subsequently mimeographed material was found by the Yugoslav police (militia) during a routine search of an automobile belonging to an East European diplomat which had been involved in a traffic violation. The documents were taken to a police station, where a sharp-eyed official noticed a discrepancy between the jargon used in the text and that which is officially sanctioned in Yugoslavia. The seizure resulted in a massive investigation, which led to the trial of the 32 men.

In the West, the text of what is occasionally referred to as the Bar Manifesto was distributed by two leading Cominformists, Perović and Bogdan Jovović, who were connected with Kiev University and the Cominformist training center there until October 1975, when it was decided that they would be much more useful in disseminating anti-Tito propaganda in the West. The KGB originally chose Paris as their base, but the French authorities refused visas. Perović somehow managed to get to Israel and has been traveling ever since, occasionally giving press interviews attacking Tito's regime. A typical interview appeared on January 22, 1976, in the leftist Brussels weekly *Notre Temps*. Its tone corresponded to the basic theme of the Bar papers, calling for Yugoslavia's integration into the East European Council for Mutual Economic Assistance (Comecon) trading block and demanding Tito's resignation and Yugoslavia's return to "really popular socialist democracy."

The case of Bogdan Jovović is perhaps more interesting. For some reason, the Soviet authorities were determined to set him up in Paris. They discovered that a French transit visa would automatically be granted to any Soviet citizen traveling from Moscow to Katmandu, the capital of Nepal. Armed with an authorization to emigrate for "the purpose of the permanent residence in Nepal," issued by the executive committee of the Federation of Societies of the Red Cross and Red Crescent in Moscow, Jovović obtained both a Nepalese entry visa and a French transit visa. Subsequently, while in Paris, he succeeded in extending his visas. One cannot rule out the possibility that the authorization to grant him temporary residence was made with the full knowledge of the French counterintelligence service, which would thus be placed in an unusually good position for monitoring the activities of the anit-Tito exiles.

The language used in the Bar papers is clearly that of classic Soviet-style pronouncements, full of accusations and often crude epithets. There are periodic references to Tito's regime as a "watchdog of American imperialism," to the "great Soviet Union," "the glorious Red Army," and the economic sins of Tito's regime. But in the torrent of often grotesque jargon and crude appeals to various groups "wronged" by Tito's regime, there are some truths with which many Western analysts tend to agree.

One can dismiss such statements as "Marshal Tito's personal dictatorship has from the very start practiced the most brutal terrorism known in the history of mankind"; or "the whole of Yugoslavia has been turned into a huge concentration camp"; or the charges that the basis of Yugoslavia's foreign policy is a "satellite-subjugation to American imperialism." But it is difficult to disregard statements that point to obvious flaws, weaknesses, and injustices of the system.

Few Yugoslavs would deny the Cominformists' claims that a majority of recent members have joined the LCY for personal gain. Equally, no one can deny Tito's overwhelming and uncontested role in the system which the Cominformists describe as "a counterrevolutionary regime based on personal power." One of the Bar papers speaks thus of Tito's role:

> The enormous powers stemming from the fusion of legislative and executive power in Tito's hands have enabled him to enforce an absolute personal dictatorship. By his assumption of powers that are not subject to control by the National Assembly, he is in a position to take any measures he considers necessary in any department of domestic or foreign policy. Elected for life, he is responsible to no one. . . .

The document gives a list of prisons and camps where it claims that political offenders are held, adding the astounding charge that "imprisoned members of the Gestapo" are instrumental in introducing tortures compared to which Nazi concentration camps "were mere clinics." But the statement that "the secret police have penetrated the whole fabric of social life" in Yugoslavia is obviously true. What the Bar papers do not say is that, in this respect, Yugoslavia hardly differs from other "socialist" states.

The Cominformists correctly state that "the state policy of noninterference into economic relations has made it impossible for the working class to realize its demand that all citizens have the right to work." What they do not say is that Yugoslav economic indicators of growth of national income and the general standard of living have been higher than those of the Soviet satellites (with the possible exception of East Germany).

The statement that the Yugoslav leaders "have been trying to solve the problem of unemployment by simply exporting [labor] to the capitalistic states" is also reasonably accurate. Obviously, the Yugoslav government does not "export" labor but merely allows the unemployed or more enterprising members of the labor pool free access to West European employment markets. The Cominformists' analysis of the impact of this situation can hardly be argued with: "The export of manpower has, on the one hand, reduced the danger of social unrest. . . . on the other hand, it has made possible a huge inflow of foreign currency into the Titoist state."

The Bar papers describe in pathetic terms the conditions of life and work of Yugoslavia's variou social groups. Again here and there, there are bits of truth: the necessity to seek work outside the country, the steep inflation rate, and the comparatively low salaries that have to some extent sapped the faith of the population in the Titoist workers' self-management. Perhaps it should be noted here that the reporting of the Yugoslav economic picture by the Soviet embassy in Belgrade centers mainly on the "moral degradation" represented by economic emigration, dissatisfaction with high prices and low wages, and other imperfections of the system. Needless to say, despite these factors, most Yugoslavs consider themselves much better off than the citizens of other East European countries. In this respect, while the Bar Manifesto can appeal to some disgruntled elements rejected by the Titoist machine, its popular appeal is bound to be limited.

Perhaps the most revealing segment of the Bar documents is contained in Part Four, dealing with the aims and objectives of the Communist Party of Yugoslavia. The heading of the chapter is blunt enough: "Liquidation of the Counterrevolutionary Regimes Based on Personal Power and Construction of a Communist Society." A 12-point program (which is mentioned in Perović's *Notre Temps* interview) calls for the dissolution of Tito's LCY and the creation of a "united People's Front of all socialist, democratic, and progressive parties, groups, and currents with an anit-Titoist orientation. . . . " It demands the "formation of a provisional government composed of parties, organizations, groups, and currents taking part in the overthrow of Tito's dictatorship" and the "abolition of the federal, republican, provincial, and communal national assemblies and the formation of commissariats of a provisional government. . . ."

Furthermore, the program proposes the "disbandment of the State Security Service and the counterintelligence organizations of the Yugoslav People's Army," abolition of the post of the president of the republic, and the enactment of measures "to permit nationalization of the principal means of production; state control over the distribution of raw materials, equipment, . . . as [well as] control over trade, prices, and credits." In short, the program is a blueprint for Yugoslavia's return to classical communism, a dramatic end to the concept of self-management and Tito's socialist market economy.

Just how do the Cominformists propose to achieve this end in a tightly controlled state in which most citizens are believed reasonably happy with its comparatively benign–by Communist standards–economic and political policies? After all, most Yugoslavs, although critical–and often bitterly so–of various facets of Titoism, take considerable pride in the fact that they can travel abroad, buy Western products, and enjoy a degree of self-expression which does not exist in many other socialist countries.

The answer is reasonably straightforward. "In order to achieve this goal," the program stipulates, "it is necessary to achieve first the fighting unity of all the sociopolitical forces of the social democratic and progressive anti-Titoist groups. Success depends on the united activity of communist-internationalists, the working class, and the broad popular masses." But it warns that "much depends . . . on the behavior of the Yugoslav People's Army and other organs of tyranny which for a long time have accepted Tito as the protector of the interests of the people. . . ." Thus, the Cominformists clearly recognize the Yugoslav army–perhaps the best organized and most nationally integrated force in Yugoslavia–as the main obstacle to their and the Soviet Union's designs. And they warn, "A new civil war can be avoided only if a broad People's Anti-Titoist Front is created in Yugoslavia with the avowed aim of introducing a new order."

The document concludes, on a comparatively grim note, that the overthrow of Tito "without a new civil war is far from easy." If the country is plunged into civil war, "full responsibility . . . would fall exclusively on the counterrevolutionary regime based on personal authority."

As one way of fostering their aim, the Cominformists propose–in a manner more exploratory than concrete–"a general strike that could paralyze the dictatorship and bring about freedom and democracy by peaceful means. Such a task is not at all easy and can be achieved only by united efforts on the part of all socialist, democratic, and progressive forces in Yugoslav society."

In general, most observers dismiss the possibility of a successful Cominformist-inspired rising, much less any intensified political agitation, as long as Tito is alive and the security apparatus firmly in control. The situation would change dramatically, however, if, in the post-Tito years, national, economic, and political pressures start rocking the foundations of Titoism.

It should be stressed at this point that Yugoslavia managed to survive enormous problems and tensions after its break with Moscow, but that when the threat of direct Soviet intervention or "punishment" became less acute, the nationality problems–with claims, quarrels, and disruptive regional interests–almost immediately came to the fore. The big question which cannot be answered in the foreseeable future is whether Tito's successor or successors can sufficiently galvanize the various nationalities of the federation to ward off the internal and external threats to Yugoslavia.

The possibility and form of Soviet intervention will be based on two main conditions: Yugoslavia's internal situation in the post-Tito years and the broader contest of international relations. Yugoslav officials tend to be optimistic, at least in their contacts with Western diplomats and political analysts. If Romanian

President Ceausescu succeeded in defying Moscow, why shouldn't Tito's successors be able to do the same? is one of the standard phrases one is likely to hear in Belgrade. But Romania, despite its large Hungarian minority and the problems of Bessarabia, does not have such a potentially disruptive national problem as Yugoslavia. Neither is it a rebel in the sociopolitical sense to the extent Yugoslavia has been. There are obvious limits to Romania's independent stance. The existence of a common frontier with the Soviet Union and the exposed Black Sea coastline are sufficient reasons for the Romanian leaders to watch their step.

Compared with Romania, control of Yugoslavia seems more vital despite Romanian oil production: Yugoslavia's strategic position, uranium deposits, the Dalmatian coastline, and its hitherto successful impact on the Third World would be enormous dividends.* Whether or not Tito's successors will be men of similar if not greater stature than Ceausescu seems immaterial.

There has been some speculation in the West concerning Moscow's conviction as to the limits of NATO's reaction in the event of Soviet interference in Yugoslavia. According to such speculation, Moscow seems reasonably convinced that Western reaction, on the whole, would not amount to much. If that is, indeed, Moscow's current assessment, it would tend to imply that the Soviet Union's behavior concerning post-Tito Yugoslavia may be much bolder than is generally believed. Still, some Western chanceries feel that historically the Soviet leadership has always been cautious when faced with situations difficult to cope with, with issues that are not clear-cut.

Moscow's alleged conviction that the West's reaction to Yugoslavia's problems would at best be limited has affected some Yugoslav officials. It has spawned the theory that since the country cannot count on effective outside help, perhaps the easiest course of action would be a modus vivendi with the USSR. This would certainly imply gradual and increasing Soviet interference in Yugoslav affairs, eventually resulting in the country's return into the Soviet fold. Whether or not such a scenario would be accompanied by turmoil depends on the unity of the army and the effectiveness of the security apparatus.

In this respect, President Carter's campaign statement that U.S. security would not be involved in the event of Soviet intervention in Yugoslavia was seen by some chanceries as giving the Soviets carte blanche to deal with Belgrade the way they see fit. A number of Western analysts agree that the net result of Carter's statement was to strengthen the pro-Soviet faction within the Yugoslav leadership and weaken the hesitant faction. Although presidential acts

---

*According to Yugoslav press reports, Yugoslavia possesses enough uranium deposits to provide the basic fuel for its planned production of nuclear power. The size of Yugoslavia's uranium deposits has never been officially estimated. Periodic references to uranium have caused speculation on the part of some West German newspapers as to whether Yugoslavia's atomic program was limited to peaceful uses.

do not always follow campaign promises, many Yugoslavs apparently became convinced that in the event of any difficulties with the Soviet Union, they would be left entirely on their own.

The publicity given early in 1976 to the so-called Sonnenfeldt doctrine—the view expressed by the then Secretary of State Henry Kissinger's aide Helmut Sonnenfeldt that a closer organic relationship between the USSR and its satellites would not be against Western interests—was greeted in Belgrade with considerable alarm. No amount of U.S. explanation that Washington considers Yugoslavia to be outside the Soviet zone of influence has managed to dispel Yugoslav fears. Belgrade clearly feels that the two superpowers are prone to "make deals" and that Yugoslavia might become one of the victims.

NOTES

1. Jerry F. Hough, "The Brezhnev Era: The Man and the System," *Problems of Communism*, March-April 1976, p. 1.
2. New York *Times*, November 27, 1976.
3. Quoted in the *Financial Times*, November 19, 1976.

CHAPTER 5
BETWEEN EAST AND WEST

Yugoslav Communism significantly influenced changes in Communism itself, but did not fundamentally influence either international relationships or non-Communist workers' movements.

Milovan Djilas
in *The New Class*

Few of the world's statesmen have matched Tito's energy and drive in the field of international relations. Even in 1976, the marshal appeared undaunted by his advanced age. His liver ailment, announced in September, merely curtailed for a time, but did not put an end to, his activities.

There are strong reasons for Tito's efforts on the world scene. The Old Partisan wants to institutionalize Yugoslavia's concept of nonalignment, to make his country into a respected arbiter of international issues and a model to be emulated by smaller Third World nations. The obvious dividends of such a policy would be an increase in Yugoslavia's stature abroad and an added encouragement to the feuding national groups to pull together at home. Tito's tireless activity in his last years is viewed by some observers as part of his effort to instill in his feuding compatriots a sense of purpose and destiny that would become a unifying factor.

On the whole, Tito's concept of Yugoslavia's role and its many-angled foreign policy is hardly commensurate with the country's size or, for that matter, leverage possibilities. Still, using his unquestionable ability, shrewdness, and the appeal of nonalignment against the designs of the big powers, Tito has succeeded in carving out for his country an important niche in the history of world diplomacy. It is reasonable to assume, however, that while his successors may try to continue Tito's blueprint, Yugoslavia's impact on world affairs will be dramatically curtailed.

Tito's aim in international relations has consisted of efforts to restrict the influence of the two power blocs and enhance that of the small, developing, and nonaligned nations. He has skillfully capitalized on the hostility of many Third World nations toward what is frequently referred to as American imperialism. In general, while attacking the United States and its allies, Tito has been much less vocal against the Soviet Union and Soviet policies. More often than not, while promoting nonalignment, Yugoslavia has also tried to promote its own brand of socialism. Hardly any of the men who are mentioned as the marshal's heirs apparent show signs or promise of being capable of projecting the same image on the international scene. The juggling for power and influence in the Yugoslav political apparatus, the sharpening of the nationality issue, and the growing Soviet pressures expected to face Yugoslavia after Tito are hardly factors which encourage an imaginative or active foreign policy. Above all, the new leaders are not likely to have anything resembling Tito's authority either at home or abroad. It is thus quite possible that Tito's frenetic diplomatic efforts in his last years may be Yugoslavia's last of such magnitude. And lacking a dimension in its diplomacy, Yugoslavia may be less capable of facing the host of problems looming before the country's new leadership. Deprived of international prestige and the drama of nonaligned initiatives, the Yugoslav federation may not look quite as appealing to those national groups harboring thoughts of greater autonomy. Even the most ardent of Tito's supporters admit that Yugoslavia's impact on the world scene can be maintained only "on the basis of national unity." That, however, is the biggest unknown factor of the post-Tito era.

It is quite significant that to the world at large, Yugoslavia's diplomacy and foreign policy are invariably associated with Tito's name. The sincerely naive question of a newly accredited African ambassador in Belgrade, "Does this country have a foreign minister, too?" shows that to many smaller nations the name Tito and Yugoslavia's political independence are the same thing.

A cursory look at the marshal's travels and efforts in the first eight months of 1976 shows how hard he has worked at his nonalignment concept. He held a dozen summit meetings involving far-ranging travel; participated in the Berlin congress of Communist party heads and the nonaligned summit at Colombo, Ceylon; offered to mediate a host of delicate international issues including the Cyprus problem, the Greco-Turkish dispute over the Aegean oil deposits, and the frontier feuds between Algeria and Morocco, Ethiopia and Somalia, Libya and Egypt. By year's end, little if anything concrete had emerged from these efforts except a rash of headlines and photographs of the aging marshal on his globe-trotting missions. In the second half of 1977, having apparently overcome the effects of his liver trouble, Tito planned more trips. They included the Soviet Union, North Korea, and the People's Republic of China (PRC).

The cornerstone of Tito's philosophy is nonalignment, a concept of considerable attraction to the proliferating, often impecunious and disoriented new nations, desperately searching for a formula that will allow them to be heard. And Tito has been telling them exactly what they want to hear: there should be no monopoly of power and influence, no deals between the blocs. The fact that Yugoslavia has often pursued a policy similar to that of Moscow has apparently not tarnished Tito's effort. What Tito has succeeded in accomplishing is to give Yugoslavia a reasonably strong political position among the developing nations without any lasting obligation. That, too, can be appealing.

One of the pioneers of the movement that would enhance the role of Third World countries vis-a-vis the power blocs, Yugoslavia has elaborated a series of principles governing membership in the nonaligned group. According to these principles, a nonaligned country must (1) adopt an independent policy based on the coexistence of states having different political systems; (2) refrain from membership in a multilateral military alliance under the hegemony of either of the power blocs;* (3) refuse military bases to foreign powers except in cases where such facilities have nothing to do with bloc rivalry; (4) support all movements for national independence.

While some so-called nonaligned nations have been interpreting these principles with considerable leeway, Yugoslavia itself has adhered to them reasonably strictly. The distinctly "socialist" orientation of the Yugoslav philosophy, however, has also had an impact on its nonalignment. For example, Yugoslavia tends to support any military dictator of a Third World country as long as he proclaims himself a "socialist." But there is some confusion concerning the Yugoslav definition of a "progressive." Thus, a Yugoslav citizen who believes in the abolition of a one-party monopoly would be described not as "progressive" but as "reactionary." Any country which opposed "American imperialism" invariably deserves the label "nonaligned and progressive." Any country hostile to the establishment of socialism is frequently identified with "American imperialism."

The impact of Yugoslav foreign policy would not have been the same had Tito restricted himself to an active role only among the countries of the Third World. Consequently, an equally vigorous effort has been pursued on the European scene. The objective is to convince Europe of the "universality of nonalignment," a phrase used by Acimović of the Institute of International Politics and Economics. It is highly questionable, however, whether such a pragmatic man as Tito really believes that nonalignment could appeal to Western Europe. Still, the concept represents a justification of what is known as Titoism. Its founder could hardly do anything else.

In contrast to the passive neutrality of such countries as Austria, Finland, or Switzerland, Yugoslavia has always sought an active if not leading role on the European scene. The European Security Conference, the Balkan meetings, the

---

*Alliances are allowed as long as they have nothing to do with either the Warsaw Pact or NATO.

Law of the Sea Conference, and the United Nations Conference on Trade and Development (UNCTAD) are some of the forums where Yugoslav delegates arrive armed with an impressive array of proposals and initiatives. The fact that most such proposals seldom go beyond the stage of initial speeches has not deterred Tito and his lieutenants from further effort. Among the swelling ranks of diplomats, the Yugoslavs have been among the most energetic. It looks as though the country fears that silence of lack of ideas on the international scene might indicate Titoism's decline.

While trying to juggle East and West, lead the nonaligned, and create an appealing image in Western Europe, Tito has devoted much of his effort to the concept of Balkan cooperation. It is easy to see why: Yugoslav planners and policy makers believe that of all the traditional political zones of the European continent, the Balkans offer the greatest potential for instability and big-power interference.

An interesting analysis of the Balkan problem as seen by Yugoslavia was made in the spring of 1976 by Petković of the *Review of International Affairs*. According to Petković, ". . . the Balkans have always exercised magnetic attraction for the great powers." Only the risk of a larger interbloc conflict has prevented the growth of this interest. As time goes by, it is becoming more obvious–again according to this theory–that "the great powers are free to act in local regions without fear that a nuclear clash would automatically ensue." Petković believes that the Balkans are in fact an area "where a move by one side need not necessarily engender a response from the other side."*

Is this a somber view by an official Yugoslav writer of the events likely to face Yugoslavia once the country is deprived of Tito's leadership? Certainly it would seem so, although more explicit speculation has been taboo in Belgrade for years. Consequently, the concept of "hands off the Balkans" is the most logical part of Titoist reasoning. According to it, only the presence of a strong, nonaligned, and internationally respected Yugoslavia can keep the big powers out and secure the area's unmolested survival.

This expression of Yugoslavia's political importance apart, it is clear that the area, where not so long ago war was more frequent than peace, has been unusually tranquil in recent years. Inevitably, there are countless latent tensions, and the various splits, doctrinaire arguments, and claims certainly do not forecast a continuation of the status quo. While Yugoslavia, Albania, and to some extent Romania can be regarded as rebels against Soviet domination, Greece and Turkey have not been particularly acquiescent allies of the United States. The potentially explosive Greco-Turkish feud and the general atmosphere

---

*The text of Petković's article, which appeared originally in the *Review of International Affairs*, has been translated into English and has been made available to foreign diplomats, newsmen, and researchers, indicating a considerable degree of official backing of his theory.

of tension in the Mediterranean represent a continuing diplomatic challenge to both superpowers. Only well-policed Bulgaria, a solid ally of Moscow, has not provided any surprises. Yet Bulgaria is ready to make its claim to Yugoslav Macedonia almost any time Moscow gives the green light, and Albania's future after the death of Hoxha is as murky as Yugoslavia's. Thus, the overall prospects for the Balkans are hardly reassuring.

The very nature of the Balkan states, divided into pro-Soviet, pro-PRC, pro-Western, and nonaligned nations, would seem to spell trouble. It is clear that any effort at viable Balkan multilateral cooperation is doomed to failure, as Tito himself has seen. He has therefore concentrated on promoting bilateral pacts with Romania, Greece, and Turkey, firmly believing that this approach can help keep the tension down. Particularly in recent years, Belgrade has been stressing Yugoslavia as a "Balkan nation" and the need for, if not some kind of unity, then at least stronger cooperation.

A Balkan policy based on bilateral relations has to take into account the specific problems of each country involved. There are very limited prospects indeed for any cooperation with Albania, a country which has barricaded itself behind minefields in its mountain fortress, with the PRC as its only ally. Even Tito himself has not come up with any initiative that would make a dent in the Albanian wall of suspicion and xenophobia. Yet in recent months the Yugoslav foreign-policy planners have been watching Albania with increased interest if not concern. During much of 1976, the little country was in the throes of considerable political upheaval. There were purges in the army on charges of pro-Moscow "revisionism." The ministers of agriculture and cultural affairs were replaced by two comparatively unknown women, and there were appeals to young people to return to the villages. Hoxha and his closest political associate, Prime Minister Shehu, were both reported ill. The PRC had cut its aid to approximately half of the usual $100 million annually, and the stream of high-powered PRC delegations had subsided to a mere trickle of comparatively low-ranking officials. One explanation for the tension in Sino-Albanian relations was that Albania had refused to follow the PRC's policy of opening its doors to the West. Another was the PRC's own internal difficulties, which limited the scope of Peking's interest in Albania and put the brakes on its largesse.*

What alarmed the Yugoslavs most was the revival of the reviosionist scare by the Albanian regime. It is very similar to Yugoslavia's own Cominformist problem, and it brings up another thorny question close to home: what will happen to Albania once the old and ailing Hoxha is no longer on the scene?

*The seventh congress of the Albanian Communist party, held in Tirana November 1-7, 1976, hinted at the existence of strained relations between Albania and the PRC. Although the congress paid tribute to the late Mao Tse-tung, Hoxha, in his keynote speech, refrained from the usual praise of the PRC, in particular ignoring its new leadership.

Should the revisionist faction get the upper hand, pushing Albania back into the Soviet camp, the pressure against Yugoslavia's independence would be even more acute. (Conversely, Yugoslavia's return to Soviet-style communism would be seen with alarm by the present Albanian leaders.) The two countries have a lot at stake in preserving their present forms of government. Yet in 1976 there were no signs of any rapprochement between Belgrade and Tirana that could, perhaps, provide an additional guarantee against internal and external pressures.

Of no small concern is the presence of the large Albanian minority in Yugoslavia, discussed in Chapter 3. The return of Soviet influence to Albania might provide an additional magnet to the estimated 1.4 million Yugoslav Albanians. Such reasoning is based on the assumption that a pro-Soviet Albania would considerably relax its internal policies, thus further heightening the aspirations toward Albanian unity frequently demonstrated among Kosovo Albanians. As it is, there are severe strains in the relationship between Albanians and Serbs within the autonomous region of Kosovo. Albania's political isolation has acted as a strong deterrent to any pro-Tirana orientation of the Kosovo Albanians. But this could change if Tirana toed the Moscow line. The prospect for Belgrade would hardly be enviable.

Of all the Balkan countries, Bulgaria alone has remained a staunch ally of the Soviet Union. This alignment is faithfully reflected in the state of Bulgarian-Yugoslav relations: when the curve of the wobbly Moscow-Belgrade dialogue points downward, it is a safe guess, as noted earlier, that a similar trend will prevail on the Belgrade-Sofia chart.

The two countries have an important and potentially dangerous bone of contention: Macedonia, now a republic within the Yugoslav federation, where a portion of the population has preserved certain sympathies for Bulgaria. Macedonia was an independent state until 1018. Subsequently, it fell under Byzantine rule and then under Turkish occupation. During the "Turkish period," the area was ruled first by Bulgarian and then by Serbian monarchs. In the latter part of the nineteenth century, revolutionary tendencies gained ground, symbolized by the strongly nationalist Internal Macedonian Revolutionary Movement (VMRO), founded mainly to oppose the Ottoman Turks. After the Balkan wars of 1912 and 1913, the area was divided among Serbia, Greece, and Bulgaria. This division has roughly persisted until now. When Yugoslavia adopted its present federal system the Yugoslav portion of Macedonia was given the status of a republic.

Before the end of World War II, Bulgaria's policy was simple: there was no Macedonian nation, and the area should revert to Bulgaria. This changed radically, most likely at Moscow's behest, after 1945, when Bulgaria reluctantly recognized that a special Macedonian national group did indeed exist. But the policy was reversed after Tito's break with the Cominform, to be changed, once again, in 1972.

Recently, there have been no formal Bulgarian territorial demands on Yugoslavia. But Sofia's recurring view that there is no Macedonian nation strikes directly at the carefully nurtured Yugoslav concept. It would seem that as far as the Macedonian problem is concerned, the Soviets have left some leeway to Sofia. Perhaps it is a safety valve, allowing some expression for Bulgarian nationalism.

The Yugoslav view of Bulgaria's overall political performance on the Balkan scene is not a flattering one. In conversations with Western diplomats, journalists, and analysts (the author included), Yugoslav officials describe Bulgaria as a block in the path of Balkan unity and cooperation. Failure to get the much-talked-about Balkan cooperation scheme beyond the stage of slogans is invariably blamed on Sofia's unconditional obedience to Moscow.*

Relations with Romania, a country with a tough internal regime but which exercises some leeway in foreign policy, have been much more relaxed and even friendly. Romania and Yugoslvia both insist on the right to "separate roads to socialism." Any Romanian effort along these lines invariably receives Yugoslav backing. On the other hand, Romanian support for Yugoslav foreign policy has been much more circumspect, for obvious geopolitical reasons.

Perhaps the most promising field for Yugoslav diplomacy in the Balkans is offered by Greece and Turkey. Although both of these countries are members of NATO, their relationship with each other and the alliance has been subject to numerous strains. The Greek-sponsored coup d'etat in Cyprus on July 15, 1974, triggered the Turkish invasion of that independent Mediterranean island, prompting the Greek regime to take its forces out of the NATO command. The subsequent U.S. pressures on Turkey, including a temporary arms embargo, paralyzed the operations of 26 highly sensitive U.S. bases on the Turkish mainland, which gathered an estimated 35 percent of U.S. electronic intelligence from the Soviet Union. Thus, NATO's southern flank is a shaky proposition. That is why Tito, with his concept of nonalignment aimed against the two power blocs, has seen fertile ground for his ideas in both Greece and Turkey.

Yugoslavia's efforts at closer cooperation with Greece and Turkey are not new. In 1954, the three countries signed what has been called the Balkan Pact. It was a mutual assistance treaty among the three, and its wording resembled that of the initial NATO pact. In the view of some strategists, the Balkan Pact would be the logical way to justify NATO's intervention in the event of any attack against Yugoslavia.

The background of the treaty is curious enough. Yugoslav initiatives aimed at Greece and Turkey in 1954 followed a period of considerable normalization

---

*For example, after the inconclusive Balkan conference held in Athens January 26-February 5, the Zagreb daily *Vjesnik* of February 8 criticized the Bulgarian delegates for preventing "any continuity in the cooperation among the Balkan countries."

in Belgrade's relations with Moscow and its satellites. Yet it would seem that the Yugoslavs regarded such a normalization with suspicion and at the same time sought some form of reassurance in the military treaty.

The treaty was signed "amid diplomatic pomp and cirucumstance"[1] at Bled, Yugoslavia, on August 9, 1954. Its terms stipulated that an aggression against one was an act of aggression against all. Article 2 of the Balkan Pact was patterned on Article 5 of the North Atlantic Treaty;

> The contracting parties have agreed that any armed aggression against one, or several of them, at any part of their territories, shall be considered as an aggression against all the contracting parties, which, in consequence, exercising the right of legitimate individual or collective defence, recognized by Article 51 of the United Nations Charter, shall individually or collectively render assistance to the party or parties attacked, undertaking in common accord and immediately all measures, including the use of armed force, which they shall deem necessary for efficacious defence.
>
> The contracting parties, with the reserve to Article 7 of the present Treaty [providing for close cooperation with the United nations], commit themselves not to conclude peace or any other arrangement with the aggressor, unless they should have previously reached common accord among themselves.[2]

The treaty, signed for a 20-year-period, was acclaimed by a number of Western governments as a significant political cold war victory. Some diplomats even hoped–publicly–that Yugoslavia would join NATO. Predictably, the Yugoslavs took a dim view of such Western wishful thinking, which was damaging to both the Yugoslav concept of nonalignment and the country's commitment to socialism. It should be remembered that at the time the Bled treaty was signed, Tito's "separate road to socialism" had existed for only six years and was still on shaky ground. Tito's closest associates, while loyal to the marshal, were never completely happy about Yugoslavia's dependence on Western, mainly U.S., arms and Western economic aid.

The record was straightened out by Tito himself in a speech on September 19, 1954. "Do not make of us what we are not," the Yugoslav leader told the West. "We are Communists." A day later Tito was even more explicit:

> The Atlantic pact is increasingly becoming painted with a political, that is, an ideological color–its fight against Communism. They say it is just against Soviet Communism, but it is more than that. . . . We are painted with a socialist complexion, and there is no room for us in a bloc which has an anti-socialist tendency.[3]

Today the most interesting thing about the treaty is that few Yugoslav officials care to comment on it officially. In fact, since the 1955 improvement in

Belgrade-Moscow relations, the Yugoslavs have generally considered the Balkan Pact a dead letter, although it has never been abrogated. Since the pact's expiration in August 1974, no legal steps have been taken by any of the signatories to terminate it. From a strictly legal point of view, this means that the pact remains valid. The Yugoslav government, however, in rare comments on the pact, has expressed the view that Yugoslavia's role as "the leader of the nonaligned world, free of all blocs, is inimical to any links with other military blocs."[4] No consultative talks of a military nature between the three Balkan Pact countries have taken place since 1955. In 1961, a Yugoslav government spokesman claimed that the pact was "dead" and that Yugoslavia was ready to take steps to formally cancel it. The statement was not published in the Yugoslav media, and no such steps have been taken.

It is significant that among its demands, the "Bar congress" of the underground Cominformist party called for the repudiation of the Balkan Pact. It can thus be assumed that the Cominformists–and their Soviet backers–are clearly concerned about the 23-year-old agreement, which has rarely figured in subsequent diplomatic conversations.

In 1976, Tito traveled to both Greece and Turkey, again offering to mediate in their age-old feud. The marshal also tried to explore the possibilities of solving the question of divided Cyprus, where the Turkish army has occupied close to 40 percent of the island's territory since 1974. Yet Tito should know better: no amount of outside pressure or persuasion is likely to have any impact on Turkey. All such efforts by the Western powers have proved counterproductive. There is little likelihood that Yugoslavia could succeed where U.S. diplomacy with its powerful leverage failed.

In his talks with Turkish Premier Suleyman Demirel, Tito, as usual, put heavy stress on nonalignment. According to Belgrade's *Politika*, "Ankara showed interest in this subject."[5] Neither the speeches made during Tito's visit nor the official joint communiqué, however, mentioned nonalignment. As usual, the Ankara visit did not achieve any substantial results. Optimists, however, saw in it yet another step toward strengthening Balkan relations, particularly in view of Turkey's difficulties with the United States.

In the spring of 1976, Ankara and Washington signed an agreement calling for a $1-billion military aid package to Turkey over a period of four years. At the end of the year, the agreement had yet to be approved by Congress. (Conscious of the strength of the so-called Greek lobby in Congress, the Ford administration proceeded to promise a $700-million aid package to Greece*)

---

*On December 2, 1976, the New York *Times* quoted parts of President-elect Carter's remarks to members of the Senate Foreign Relations Committee in which he said he hoped the United States would ratify the agreements with Turkey and Greece to "continue an adequate military presence in those countries." The newspaper also quoted Carter as saying that U.S. bases in Turkey were important and the presence of the U.S. fleet in the Eastern Mediterranean was "crucial."

The Turks, needless to say, have shown little patience for the nuances of U.S. internal politics, and in the autumn of 1976 there were periodic calls in Turkey in favor of pulling out of NATO. On December 1, Prime Minister Demirel described the 1975 U.S. arms embargo as a hostile act and complained that his country was lacking essential spare parts for its U.S. hardware. Opposition leader Bulent Ecevit has hinted privately on several occasions that perhaps Turkey should follow in Greece's footsteps and take its forces out of NATO's command. After the June 5th, 1977 general elections in Turkey, which allowed Ecevit to form a government, such statements took on a much more concrete meaning. Against such a background, it is not surprising to see Tito's efforts to exploit the disenchantment of a NATO country for the vague purpose of creating a nonaligned Balkan zone against both blocs.

The Balkan-cooperation theme was equally stressed during Tito's visit to Athens, which preceded that to Turkey. There again, it was a matter of words rather than concrete acts. The obvious question is, if Tito with his charisma and appeal has been unable to make a deeper impact on the Balkan scene, how can his heirs succeed? The answer, most likely, will be that Yugoslavia's Balkan initiatives after Tito will be hardly more than nonstarters–just as Tito's have been.

Despite such efforts in the Balkans, the Yugoslav government claimed as late as 1976 that it had "no special Balkan policy." According to one official foreign office spokesman, "Yugoslavia has no special policy because it has a unified global concept of its nonalignment policy. The Yugoslav concept of nonalignment is not and can never be compatible with any separate concept of Balkan policy which would be based on some special postulates." In view of the rhythm of the country's Balkan diplomacy, including Tito's personal travels, it was a somewhat strange statement. While Tito was stressing Yugoslavia's Balkan role, his officials were still insisting that Yugoslavia "has emerged from the narrow Balkan context into the world scene as an active participant in global affairs."[6]

At the same time, foreign office spokesmen were admitting that things had not gone quite as expected on the European scene after the 1975 Helsinki summit meeting of 35 nations directly involved with European security which effectively ratified the European borders set up in the wake of World War II. Although the Yugoslavs described Helsinki as a "milestone" and in 1977 hosted a working level session to implement the human rights provisions of the 1975 summit, many Yugoslav officials saw a clear discrepancy between the intentions voiced in the Finnish capital and the deeds that followed. The best the Yugoslav foreign office could say was that "there have been trends not conforming to the spirit of Helsinki. In fact, many moves seem to be aimed at strengthening the division of Europe."

It was not a veiled accusation aimed at the Soviet Union. The culprit was the United States, or more specifically what has been generally referred to as the Sonnenfeldt doctrine, which, despite U.S. denials and a subsequent strong statement by then Secretary of State Kissinger in London, the Yugoslavs regarded in 1976 as the key to Washington's future attitude toward Eastern Europe. Six months after the advent of the Carter administration, the Yugoslavs were still unsure whether Washington was weighing any major policy changes toward their part of the world.

The disclosure by the U.S. press of State Department counselor Sonnenfeldt's confidential remarks before a meeting of U.S. ambassadors in London in December, 1975, shattered Belgrade's confidence in itself. It smelled of "another Yalta"; it showed the vulnerability of Yugoslav foreign policy; it struck at the very heart of Titoism. If there were in Belgrade, in the spring of 1976, officials inclined to "make a deal" with Moscow, their political judgment must have been looked at in a new light.

What exactly cast a pall of gloom over the satellite capitals, and particularly over the foreign ministry in Belgrade, after the disclosure of Sonnenfeldt's statement? An analysis of the text of his remarks, distributed by the U.S. Department of State, as well as conversations with two ambassadors who participated in the meeting shows that it would be presumptuous to consider the Sonnenfeldt statement a "doctrine." His analysis of the situation in Eastern Europe, seen in light of the relations between East and West and between the Soviet Union and its client states, basically recommends that Soviet control of the eastern half of Europe be regarded as a reality and be dealt with as such. If détente in Europe is to survive, Sonnenfeldt argued, then it is better for all concerned that the Soviets have a more normal relationship with their satellites.

Otherwise, as Sonnenfeldt pointed out, the desire of the East European satellites for greater separate identity might lead to a major explosion. Pointing to the USSR's inability to create links with its satellites by means other than force, Sonnenfeldt suggested that "this inorganic, unnatural relationship is a far greater danger to world peace than the conflict between East and West. . . . So it must be our policy to strive for an evolution that makes the relationship between the Eastern Europeans and the Soviet Union an organic one."

It was the bluntness of the remarks—first "leaked" to Washington columnists Rowland Evans and Robert Novak[7]—that shocked Eastern Europe. Yet the shock was caused mainly by the fact that it was the first official indication of Washington's recognition of the Soviet claims to Eastern Europe in the post-Helsinki era. As Sonnenfeldt pointed out, some countries, such as Poland and Hungary, had already adopted an extremely pragmatic attitude that had allowed them a large degree of national identity without provoking tension and Moscow's wrath. Indeed, pragmatism has become the watchword among the Poles, who, according to Sonnenfeldt, "have been able to overcome their romantic political inclinations which led to their disasters in the past."

But Belgrade is not Warsaw, Budapest, or Bucharest, least of all submissive Prague. The fact that Sonnenfeldt included Yugoslavia and its future in his statement was seen as a bad omen by Yugoslav foreign policy specialists. It mattered little that Sonnenfeldt stressed the necessity of "continuing the independence of Yugoslavia from Soviet domination." What rankled Belgrade was the subsequent sentence, saying bluntly, ". . . we accept that Yugoslav behavior will continue to be, as it has been in the past, influenced and constrained by Soviet power." It was the kind of language Belgrade is not used to. No one, as far as the Yugoslavs are concerned, should talk bluntly about their country.

Some Yugoslav officials considered it almost an act of "interference" in Yugoslavia's internal affairs. And, needless to say, the eventual distribution of the statement to the press was seen in Belgrade as a plot by the State Department to embark on an anti-Yugoslav campaign. Moreover, Sonnenfeldt's concluding remarks struck even harder at Yugoslav pride: ". . . we would like them [Yugoslavs] to be less obnoxious, and we should allow them to get away with very little. We should especially disabuse them of any notion that our interest in their relative independence is greater than their own and, therefore, they have a free ride."

The shock waves reached Tito himself. The founder of Titoism was furious, according to some informants. Yugoslavia has never been "obnoxious," he is said to have exclaimed to his aides—just nonaligned. Yugoslav policy makers see nothing wrong with attacking Washington and "American imperialism" at almost every opportunity. Yet they resent any reference to their attitude, even in the form of a confidential briefing subsequently released to the press.

About two months after the disclosure of the Sonnenfeldt remarks, talks about the purchase of $1.5 million worth of U.S. TOW antitank missiles by Yugoslavia quietly collapsed. The Yugoslavs, it was said at the time, were annoyed with the publicity the affair was getting in the U.S. media. Again, it was seen as part of a Washington plot. Despite a long and comparatively involved relationship between the two countries, most Yugoslav officials are still unable to conceive of the U.S. press as being free. Time and time again in 1975 and 1976, the foreign ministry accused Ambassador Silberman of "manipulating" the three resident U.S. correspondents in Belgrade. Silberman's angry denials—he is not a career diplomat and has behaved with considerable bluntness—were received with condescending smiles.*

Silberman did succeed in making a strong impact on the placid Belgrade diplomatic scene. When, after relentless efforts, he finally prevailed upon the Yugoslavs to release naturalized U.S. citizen Laszlo Toth from jail, where he was serving a seven-year sentence on charges of espionage, the ambassador finally gave vent to his feelings. "He is no more a spy of any kind than my Aunt Matilda or my ten-year-old daughter," he said on July 23, 1976, when Toth was safely

*On November 17, 1976, the White House announced that President Ford had accepted Ambassador Silberman's resignation. Normally, all ambassadors submit their resignation when a new president takes office. Silberman's early gesture was viewed as an attempt to ease the strained Belgrade-Washington relationship.

on an airplane after serving nearly one year of his sentence. And after recalling his difficulties with the Yugoslav government—and the State Department's East European section—over his efforts to obtain Toth's release, Silberman concluded:

> As far as I'm concerned, the release of Toth by the Yugoslav Government is a recognition on their part that we do care deeply about the capricious imprisonment of an American.
>
> And I think that's all to the good, in terms of building and solidifying our relationship with Yugoslavia.
>
> They must understand what's in our vital interest.[8]

These honest but undiplomatic words caused a near storm in Belgrade. Tito himself once again stepped into the arena, accusing the ambassador, in an interview with Tanjug, of interfering in Yugoslavia's internal affairs. "He [Silberman] is giving lessons about our internal and foreign policy and interfering in our affairs," Tito said. "This is also a part of the attempts in some way to compromise our country among the non-aligned nations. . . ." Tito, clearly, appeared convinced that the United States' aim was to reduce Yugoslavia's world role and compromise its policies.

It would seem that throughout 1976, and at least during the first six months of 1977, Yugoslavia's relationship with both the United States and the Soviet Union was far from satisfactory. In a way, it looked as if in his last years Tito did not care whether he antagonized the two countries that really matter on the world scene.

Was Tito really so confident that his stature in the Third World sufficed to challenge both superpowers? Did his frenetic but basically meaningless trips to Stockholm and Berlin, Athens, and Ankara, and dozens of other capitals really convince him that he had erected a permanent cast-iron mold for his country's foreign policy into which all others should fit?

Belgrade seemed somehow pacified when, after the shock of the Sonnenfeldt remarks, Kissinger delivered what was a comparatively strong speech on June 25, 1976, before the International Institute for Strategic Studies in London. Repeating a previously voiced stand, Kissinger warned the Soviet Union that "coexistence requires mutual restraint." And he added, "We are determined to deal with Eastern Europe on the basis of the sovereignty and independence of each of its countries. We recognize no spheres of influence and no pretensions to hegemony."[9]

Was this meant to repudiate his aide's remarks, at the same time reassuring East European capitals—and ethnic minorities at home—during a presidential election year? Probably yes.

Whatever the statement was meant to accomplish, after initial approval it created further confusion in Belgrade. The language was basically acceptable to the champions of nonalignment. But there was something that did not look right.

Which was the more correct: the private briefing for U.S. ambassadors in Europe or the statement aimed at a worldwide audience? The Yugoslavs had no answer.

It would be impossible to talk about Yugoslav-U.S. relations without mentioning the United States' role in helping Belgrade survive its 1948 break with Moscow. Between 1951 and 1959, U.S. military assistance to Yugoslavia amounted to $700 million. Economic aid—including grants, loans, and concessional sales—had topped $2 billion when the program ended in 1967. It is often argued that had it not been for the United States' vigorous backing of Belgrade's independence efforts, the Yugoslav experiment would have ended long ago. Yet few Yugoslav officials have been willing to acknowledge the degree of U.S. assistance. It is generally accepted in Yugoslavia today that U.S. aid was the result of sheer self-interest—to keep the Soviets from the heart of the Balkans. The existence of this aid—crucial at the time when Yugoslavia was struggling against the effects of its break with Moscow—has played no role in influencing Yugoslavia's foreign policy. On the contrary, in later years it has seemed as if the United States were the main enemy of Yugoslav independence and nonalignment. Attacks against Washington in the Yugoslav press are almost daily fare. While criticism of the Soviet Union is generally veiled, there is no such restraint concerning Washington. It seems that the freedom to attack the United States has become the proverbial safety valve for frustrated Yugoslav journalists.

At the same time, Washington has accepted various Yugoslav initiatives and accusations with unusual stoicism. Except for Sonnenfeldt's somewhat acerbic remarks, originally aimed at a very limited audience, there is no record of any strong public criticism of Yugoslavia by a high U.S. official. Ambassador Silberman's remarks would hardly cause a ripple in a non-Communist capital. It can be said objectively that the U.S. attitude toward Yugoslavia has been unusually gentle in the face of an often hostile policy and propaganda effort.

The confidence with which the Yugoslavs criticize the United States was considerably bolstered by Soviet recognition, at the June 1976 East Berlin congress, of "separate roads to socialism." The Yugoslav delegation, led by the tireless Tito himself, returned from the congress in a state of near euphoria. "We are no longer alone," "the French and Italian Communist parties are our allies," "the Soviet Union no longer has a monopoly on the doctrine and its interpretations," were some of the comments one heard in Belgrade early in July 1976.

Belgrade's diplomatic community was divided: some felt that the Yugoslavs, with their history of successful defiance of Moscow, were correct in their assessment. Others were more inclinded to feel that the self-centered nation once again tended to misread the future possibilities of the Soviet Union, confident of the support of the nonaligned world as well as that of the West European Communist parties. In the event of crisis, such support can be limited at best, although the approval of Yugoslavia's independent stance by West European Communists has—so far—played a certain role in moderating the Soviet Union's attitude. It has been suggested that Moscow would not risk alienating such large and important West European Communist movements as those in France and Italy by conducting a policy that could be interpreted as interference in Yugoslavia's internal affairs. That concept is debatable. In the past, when Soviet interests were at stake, no amount of criticism or indignation voiced in the West–including the Communist parties–mattered. It is logical to assume that in its attitude toward Yugoslavia, Moscow will be ultimately guided by its own considerations.

There was much talk in Belgrade in 1976 about the "Western Brezhnev doctrine"–a reference to the Soviet concept, attributed to the party chairman, asserting the Soviet Union's right to interfere if a socialist system in its zone of influence is threatened. This time, it was the Americans who, according to the Yugoslavs, wielded the threat of the Brezhnev doctrine. Secretary Kissinger's various warnings about the impact of Communist participation in the Italian government were seen in Belgrade as "showing the true colors by American imperialists."

The key to U.S. policy toward Yugoslavia has been, in the words of a State Department aide, "the support of Yugoslavia's independence, sovereignty, territorial integrity, and economic viability." The phrase "economic viability" might indicate that the United States is willing to go further than in the case of most countries. Just how far has not been publicly specified. There are no signs that U.S. aid, ended in 1967 when legislative action precluded further concessional sales of surplus agricultural commodites, is about to be resumed. Private U.S. investments in Yugoslavia so far have not played a major role in the country's economy.

Kissinger himself was said by one of his aides to have felt that "a centralized [Communist] party, a unified army, a strong and active security service, and the determination of a strong leadership are likely to keep Yugoslavia together" when Tito is no longer there. The accent on "strong and active security service" would indicate that Washington was willing to back what is basically an oppressive regime, provided Yugoslavia survives in one piece.

Not all U.S. foreign policy makers are happy with this attitude. There are some who feel that in the long run such support for Tito's–or a Titoist–regime may become cumbersome for U.S. foreign policy. After all, the repression reintroduced by Tito in his last years may well destroy the much-needed public support for his successors–assuming that the concept of Titoism survives. And the United States, once again, will be identified with support for a police state, although this time on the left of the spectrum.

Washington, on the whole, has accepted some of the more anti-U.S. accents of the Yugoslav foreign policy with considerable patience. At least during the Ford administration, the State Department espoused the theory that only Tito's Communist party–and that implies the foreign policy it created–can keep Yugoslavia together. All other alternatives, according to this view, would be doomed to failure simply because there is no democratic tradition in Yugoslavia;

the prewar political parties have long been forgotten, and the Soviet Union, in any case, would not be likely to tolerate a non-Communist regime. The economic side of Titoism—workers' self-management—has been implemented and, although far from perfect, has passed the initial test. Hence, the West—and that includes London, Bonn, and Paris in addition to Washington,—sees no valid alternative to Titoism, even after the marshal's death.

But the West does realize that Yugoslavia is more than likely to undergo significant changes in its foreign policy after Tito. The loss of charismatic leadership and appeal to the Third World, the resulting weakness on the European scene, and less leeway in maneuvering against the Soviet Union may be only the beginning. It is not inconceivable that Washington may be happy when Yugoslavia's aggressive and generally anti-U.S. policy among the nonaligned nations comes to an end. But if Belgrade moves closer to the Soviet line—as is likely—Tito's freewheeling nonalignment may be regretted. In any case, Western leverage possibilities are limited: as Sonnenfeldt pointed out, the Soviet Union is bound to exercise more influence on Belgrade than is Washington.

NOTES

1. George W. Hoffman and Fred Warner Neal, *Yugoslavia and the New Communism* (New York: Twentieth Century Fund, 1962), p. 422.

2. Denise Follett, ed., *Documents on International Affairs, 1954*, Royal Institute of International Affairs (London: Oxford University Press, 1957), p. 198.

3. Hoffman and Neal, op. cit., pp. 422-23.

4. Slobodan Stanković, "The Cyprus Crisis and the Balkan Pact," mimeographed (Munich: Radio Free Europe, August 19, 1974), p. 4.

5. June 8, 1976.

6. These remarks were made in the course of confidential interviews with the author in Belgrade, May-July, 1976.

7. Rowland Evans and Robert Novak, "A Soviet-East Europe 'Organic Union,' " Washington *Post*, March 22, 1976.

8. New York *Times*, July 24, 1976.

9. U.S., Department of State, *The Industrial Democracies: The Imperative of Cooperation*, Bureau of Public Affairs, Office of Media Services, n.d., p. 6.

CHAPTER

6

NEITHER FISH NOR FOWL

> The dilemma is whether to bring about general progress by sacrificing some part of self-management or to strengthen self-management by sacrificing some social efficiency.
>
> *Ekonomska Politika*
> Belgrade, January 21, 1967

The audience gathered in Belgrade University's auditorium sat in rapt attention. The speaker was Vladimir Bakarić, a member of the executive committee of the LCY and of the collective presidency slated to replace Tito. The date was May 27, 1976.

"We thought that self-management would create a placid society without any big problems, a society which would preserve the status quo in social events and relations," said the man generally regarded as one of Tito's key advisers and a longtime believer in economic decentralization. "This has proved an illusion. . . . I am saying this not to scare people but rather to enable them to understand better what has been going on and to begin to study more effectively political economy in Marx's sense."[1]

Six months later, in the uneasy atmosphere of a Belgrade braced for a post-Tito era, there was still no official explanation of these somewhat enigmatic words. To a number of observers the statement, coming from a man of Bakarić's stature and influence, seemed to indicate the advent of yet another change in Yugoslavia's search for a formula to combine capitalist efficiency with Marxist doctrine. To some it presaged a dramatic evolution of self-management, one of the pillars of Titoism.

The system known as workers' self-management represents to a great extent the pride of the Yugoslav government. It has impressed much of the Third World—without any sign of emulation of the Yugoslav experiment—as well as some members of the "progressive" West European intelligentsia. It has shown considerable pragmatism on the part of a country officially espousing Marxism.

But Marx was "neither a planner nor a planning expert," according to Djilas, who charges that while "in practice, nothing is done according to Marx.... The claim that planning is conducted according to Marx satisfied people's consciences and is used to justify tyranny and economic domination for 'ideal' aims and according to 'scientific' discoveries." And Djilas further expounds:

> Yugoslavia's so-called workers' management and autonomy, conceived at the time of the struggle against Soviet imperialism as a far-reaching democratic measure to deprive the party of the monopoly of administration, has been increasingly relegated to one of the areas of party work. . . . Worker's management has not brought about a sharing in profits by those who produce, either on a national level or in local enterprises. This type of administration has increasingly turned into a safe type for the regime. Through various taxes and other means, the regime has appropriated even the share of the profits which the workers believed would be given to them.[2]

There has been considerable discussion in Yugoslavia and in the West on just how responsible self-management has been for the standard of living the country now enjoys. While official propaganda likes to attribute it to the specific economic system of the country, this author traces it to four major factors: (1) massive Western (mainly U.S.) help to Yugoslavia during the difficult years which followed the break with the Cominform; (2) intensive trade with the West and Western investment in Yugoslavia; (3) the flow of Western tourists, bringing an estimated $800 million annually in hard currency; (4) the 1 million Yugoslav guest workers in Western Europe, with their hard-currency remittances and support for relatives in Yugoslavia.

A more critical view is likely to be that the system has fared as well as it has, not because of, but despite socialist self-management. In a way, the system's contradictions and oscillation have created a serious conflict potential bound to confront Tito's successors, further complicating their task.

The system has obvious flaws:

1. It is "neither fish nor fowl," equally disappointing to believers in an unhindered market economy and to orthodox communists.

2. Party interference is the ultimate weapon in the decision-making process, regardless of economic considerations and imperatives.

3. Despite some improvement, the quality of Yugoslav goods remains below Western standards, reducing the prospect of export for the much-needed hard currency and forcing Yugoslavia to seek increasing ties with the Eastern Comecon countries, where Yugoslav products are much in demand.

4. It has created large-scale corruption, practically to the degree existing in other East European countries, prompting Tito himself to threaten to take "appropriate new measures." In an interview with the Zagreb daily *Vjesnik* on February 1, 1976, referring to the popular chant, "Comrade Tito, even people who didn't steal before are stealing now," Tito promised to step up the struggle against economic crimes and abuses.

5. It has not been able to solve the unemployment problem, resorting instead to the comparatively easy and available formula of exporting labor. Consequently, the degree of Yugoslav prosperity to a large extent depends on that of the Western capitalist countries that provide employment to Yugoslav guest workers. During the 1975 recession in the West, an estimated 80,000 Yugoslav workers lost their jobs in West Germany and were forced to return to Yugoslavia, swelling the ranks of the unemployed.

6. The burden on workers of frequent meetings of the various socio-economic units has reduced productivity, while the lack of profit incentive has led to a lackadaisical attitude toward work.

Unemployment is perhaps the system's most serious problem—and there is little hope for a quick solution. In addition to the nearly 1 million Yugoslav workers in the mid-1970s employed in Western Europe, mainly Germany, 10 percent of the labor force in the public sector is jobless. Government sources indicate that 4.8 million persons were gainfully employed in 1976, or roughly 25 percent of the total population. By international standards, it is an alarmingly low figure.* It has prompted more orthodox Communists in the party apparatus to complain that the socialist market economy has blatantly flouted one of the basic principles of Marxism: the right to full employment.

Perhaps the most dangerous flaw in the system is its recourse to the export of labor to the West. Thus, in the summer of 1976 some 1 million Yugoslavs, working outside Yugoslavia, were supporting 4 million Yugoslavs in Yugoslavia itself. In short, approximately 25 percent of the Yugoslav population was being fed, as one Yugoslav economist bluntly pointed out, "by Western capitalism." A serious economic slump in the West is enough to send back the workers and consequently deprive 4 million other Yugoslavs of their means of livelihood. A recession would also affect Western tourism and trade. Unrest leading to strikes, demonstrations, and nationalist demands by the more affluent republics would be easy to imagine.

Conversely, any doubts and difficulties surrounding the transfer of power to a new generation of leaders after Tito's death are more than likely to make Yugoslavia's Western economic partners more cautious. That is why the Yugoslav authorities frown on any Western press speculation about the country's

---

*In April 1975 the labor force in the United States represented 61.2 percent of the total population, including members of the armed forces. Of this percentage, 8.6 percent were unemployed.

potential post-Tito difficulties: such speculation might easily lead to a curtailment of essential trade and Western investment. Thus, despite some positive signs on the economic horizon during 1976 after a very difficult 1975, the economic situation after Tito is likely to be considerably perturbed. To what degree the trend can be contained is hard to assess.

The system is full of contradictions: while the Yugoslav press thunders against capitalism and predicts its eventual collapse, the country's economic performance overwhelmingly depends on that of the capitalist Western economies. (It should be pointed out that the economies of other East European countries are also being increasingly tied to the West.) For political reasons, the party is pressuring the government to provide more jobs. Yet government economists try to keep the number of jobs down—simply because the system at this stage can ill afford higher employment without a higher investment rate.

The Yugoslav workers abroad are an important factor in considering the possible courses Yugoslavia's economy may take. For one thing, all of them have become accustomed to the more efficient and more remunerative system in the West. Many feel that their country could perform better under different political circumstances, and some privately suggest that only a Western-style market economy could propel Yugoslavia toward the kind of prosperity the government is promising. It is now estimated that since temporary migratory labor in the West was allowed and even encouraged, some 3 million Yugoslavs (not counting their families) have been exposed to Western methods. It is not inconceivable that these workers may one day start exerting pressure on the Yugoslav economic structure, although so far there have been no signs of such pressure.

Few workers emigrate to settle down in the West. Most simply go for a period of time to earn money, generally to build a house in the country and spend the rest of their days as farmers, reasonably free from government controls. Despite a heavy accent on industrialization and a major shift of population to urban centers since the end of World War II, the 8 million Yugoslav peasants, who own 85 percent of the agricultural land, represent some 35 percent of the population. Although there are no official statistics, the workers returning from Western Europe tend to put a brake on the trend away from the land.

Not all become farmers by choice. Many complain that the existing restrictions prevent them from investing their earnings in profitable small businesses. Their choice, basically, narrows down to farming or to the purchase of expensive consumer goods, such as automobiles, which they do not really need. This in itself is not very healthy for the economic outlook.

To prevent the returning workers from investing their money in Yugoslavia's industry seems shortsighted on the part of the regime. The effect of this policy has already been felt in more than one way. Many of the cautious guest workers have decided to keep their money in foreign banks rather than repatriate it. It has been estimated that only 40 percent of the savings of

Yugoslav workers in Western Europe finds its way home—or roughly $1 billion annually. Yugoslav accounts in West German banks alone are believed to total some DM 6 billion (about $2.5 billion)—a major sum by any standard. The Yugoslav government has been attempting to put pressure on the West Germans to transfer the funds to Yugoslavia, so far without success.

Officials steadfastly proclaim that the principle of self-management is an integral part of Titoism. As long as Tito is alive, there is no question of departing from it. That is why Bakarić's statement caused confusion. While admitting—rather reluctantly—some of its imperfections, the government insists that no changes are likely. Pašić, one of the regime's chief ideologues, said, "We do not think of alternatives but merely of improvements."

As far as most Yugoslavs are concerned, the improvements have been limited. A Yugoslav economic writer, who preferred to remain anonymous in this study, claimed that the continuation of successful self-management depends largely on a massive injection of Western capital and the total reorientation of trade Westward rather than Eastward. Such a solution, however, would be another indication of the weakness of the system. To some it would hardly seem compatible with the principle of nonalignment, another pillar of Titoism.

Most casual visitors to Yugoslavia are impressed with the obvious signs of the country's prosperity, particularly when compared to the Soviet bloc. It should be stressed here that such outward signs of affluence as well-stocked stores and the plentiful supply of luxury consumer goods are part of the official policy. Yugoslavia has had no food shortages for years, and anybody with cash does not need to shop in the West. Consequently, violent upheavals such as those which shook Poland in 1970 and, to some extent, in 1976 are not likely to happen if the present policies are continued. The Slovenian republic, in the northwestern corner of the country, hardly differs from neighboring Austria. Croatia offers an impressive image of high-rise buildings on the outskirts of its cities, modern airports at Zagreb and Dubrovnik, villas of affluent technocrats along the scenic Dalmatian coast, and latest model Mercedes-Benz automobiles crowding the highways. The obvious question is how can so many people afford such impressive possessions if their official pay scale is less than half of that in an average Western country?

The official answers are moonlighting, working wives, and help from relatives abroad. A less official explanation points to large-scale corruption, including bribes, kickbacks from foreign firms to officials negotiating contracts, and other illegal but widespread ways of securing cash, mainly from Western sources. Tito himself has made a clear distinction between legitimate investors—mainly workers returning from the West—and local profiteers. "We must know how people have acquired their property, but we must not put everyone in the same category," the marshal has said. "We must not lump together those who work hard to be able to build a house with the help of their families and those who suddenly, virtually overnight, are able to build themselves a villa. . . . Where and how did they get their money?"[3]

The situation has caused obvious hostility toward the new technocrat class, particularly among university students who are increasingly forced to seek employment outside Yugoslavia. The frequently heard student chant, "We are not beef to be exported," is indicative of the prevailing mood. This dissatisfaction affecting the young generation is an extremely dangerous factor threatening the future of self-management.

Most university graduates forced to seek menial jobs abroad simply because their country's economy has no place for their talent regard the situation as demeaning. There have been heated calls in university debates for a revision of the system. Privately, some students express the feeling that the system might as well abandon all notions of "socialism" because it has failed to live up to the cardinal pillar of all socialist systems: full or at least reasonably full employment.

Particularly affected by the difficulties plaguing the internal labor market are architects, linguists, and liberal arts graduates. Many end up working as factory hands in West Germany or Sweden, bitterly complaining about the system which raised their expectations by giving them a free education and then forced them out "into the cold." (It should be noted here that the rapid development of institutions of higher learning in Yugoslavia after World War II has produced an inordinately high number of university graduates. This symptom is not limited to Yugoslavia but is typical of all East European socialist countries.) The Yugoslav self-management system, with its intricate network of multitiered councils and overlapping bodies, happily provides employment to economists and law graduates. Lawyers, it seems, are an unusually privileged class in Tito's Yugoslavia: the author noted that a good proportion of impressive villas on the Dalmatian coast belong to people who identify themselves as lawyers.

Another possibly disruptive factor is the glaring discrepancy in the revenue and standard of living between the various republics. For example, while prosperous Slovenia boasts a per capita income of close to $1,600–and in some areas as much as $2,400–the figure for the Albanian Kosovo autonomous region is $600. The federal system, as stated previously, requires the wealthier republics to contribute to the welfare of the less developed ones. The Federal Development Fund, created in 1965, calls for a contribution equivalent to 2 percent of the taxes paid by all socially owned enterprises. The distribution of the contributions, worked out on the basis of the needs of the less developed regions, called for the following appropriation of the fund: Bosnia-Hercegovina, 30.7 percent; Kosovo, 30.0; Macedonia, 26.2; and Montenegro 13.1.

The main contributors were Croatia and Slovenia. The fact that Serbia (with the exception of the Kosovo autonomous region) did not qualify for such subsidies did not diminish nationalist feelings, particularly in Croatia. Rather than forging the Yugoslav federation, the forced contributions have been exacerbating the artificial nature of the Yugoslav state. The distribution of unemployment—which stood at 10 percent of the labor force in the public sector in 1976—also varies from republic to republic. Thus, while comparatively prosperous Slovenia claims only a 1.3 percent jobless rate, the percentage rises to 20 in such areas as Kosovo, Macedonia, and Montenegro.

The main yardstick for determining who is unemployed is figures provided by the government labor office. These figures indicate mainly persons registered as actively seeking work. They do not include the large agricultural sector in the southern portion of the country, which provides hardly more than subsistence economy. A curious fact is that in times of prosperity (Yugoslavia is invariably affected by the capitalist economic cycles), as the demand for work grows in the more active republics, the national unemployment curve shoots up. This simply means that more people have registered with the labor office in expectation of finding jobs.

The Titoist socioeconomic system has been spelled out in detail in the country's 1974 constitution. Articles 10 through 152 fully describe the elaborate system of self-managing communities, private and public ownership, the status of the working people, and other facets of self-management. It would be impossible and basically pointless to quote them at length in this study. But the basic principles should be mentioned in order to understand the guiding philosophy of the system.

Article 10 of the constitution states that

> the socialist socio-economic system of the Socialist Federal Republic of Yugoslavia shall be based on freely associated labor, socially owned means of production, and self-management by the working people in production, in the distribution of the social product of basic and other organizations of associated labor, and in social reproduction as a whole.

Article 11 further specifies that

> man's economic and social status shall be determined by labor and the results of labor on the basis of equal rights and responsibilities.
>
> No one may gain any material or other benefits, directly or indirectly, by exploiting the labor of others.
>
> No one may in any way make it impossible for a worker to decide or restrict his decision-making on an equal footing with other workers or his labor and the conditions and results of his labor.

This principle has led to a series of bizarre situations which have shackled the performance of the system, requiring the average worker to devote close to one of every five workdays to meetings that decide wage increases, remunerations for managerial personnel, and other highly technical matters. (The time spent on meetings varies from industry to industry.) It is not infrequent that cleaning women who belong to hospital self-management councils have tried to dictate standards of performance to surgeons. Such examples can be found in almost every industry and public service in Yugoslavia. The situation has created particularly difficult problems for enterprise directors. The party would like managers to have a sound understanding of the laws of a market economy and at the same time be loyal to communist ideology, which frowns upon any excessive decentralization or undue independence of enterprises. Invariably, company directors tended to be blamed for a poor economic performance. The result was an acute management crisis in 1975 and part of 1976, during which "very few people have been willing to enter the public competition for leading posts instituted by enterprises."[4] One metallurgical complex in Serbia looked for a director for 15 months, despite three public competitions.[5]

In addition to being torn between party ideology and the need to compete on the world market, Yugoslav business organization directors also have to cope with the pressures exercised by the workers' councils. While a director is theoretically regarded as part of the self-management stucture, workers frequently consider him to be outside *their* structure, not unlike the situation in Western capitalist countries. It is a dilemma to which no one has found a satisfactory answer simply because the system has decided that a conflict between management and labor does not exist in socialist Yugoslav conditions.

Ichak Adizes of the University of California at Los Angeles, an American who has been studying Yugoslav self-management for a number of years, thus summed up the incongruous situation during a Belgrade round-table discussion:

> It is difficult to talk about the efficiency of a system if one starts from the assumption that no conflict exists and that all goals are known, especially when these goals are not sufficiently defined in an operational sense. This means we know the goals but have not defined them operationally; that is why everyone who says things that are not liked by someone else can be accused of being against self-management. If directors are strong, one says this is not self-management; if directors are weak, it is also said that this is not self-management; if everyone participates, it is claimed that this is not self-management; if economic results are not good—again this is not self-management. For heaven's sake, then, what is self-management?[6]

Yet some scholars in the West feel that it is a praiseworthy system which has brought Yugoslavia closer to "pure Leninism" than any other Communist country. In his book *The Legitimation of a Revolution: The Yugoslav Case*, Denitch thus describes Yugoslavia's socioeconomic doctrine:

> . . . when one examines the outputs of the Yugoslav system, the growing tendency toward egalitarianism in Yugoslav self-management,

> the campaigns against privilege which are simply not possible in any of the other East European countries, and the latent and real social power wielded by the workers through the instruments of self-management, one can conclude, even without considering the weakness of the private sector, that Yugoslavia is probably closer to a model of what Lenin called a workers' state and Marx and Engels referred to as the dictatorship of the proletariat, than any of the regimes calling themselves communist.[7]

Few Yugoslav officials would describe their system in more enthusiastic terms. Yet in numerous interviews with blue-collar and while-collar workers, recent university graduates, and even some technocrats, the author discovered that what they talk about mainly are the imperfections of the system rather than its advantages. It is the author's conviction that a vast majority of Yugoslavs accept the system purely and simply because it has been imposed upon the country by the all-powerful party machine. Any challenge to self-management is a crime against the state, a direct threat to Titoism. Equally frowned upon are any suggestions that it would be more profitable to the country to abandon the flimsy notions of Marxism and to move squarely toward capitalism, on which Yugoslavia relies to such an overwhelming extent. But to the Titoist regime, capitalism implies "pluralism" and the eventual disintegration of the whole basis of postwar Yugoslavia. By means of his magnetic personality and the ubiquitous police surveillance, Tito has succeeded in making self-management into a dogma. It is debatable whether his successors can maintain the same impact, particularly in view of the external factors on which the economy depends to such an extent.

An analysis of how self-management works in the shipbuilding industry is quite revealing. The study was made by Ivan Segota, a Yugoslav maritime expert, and deals with the Third of May shipyard in Rijeka, which is responsible for a large share of Yugoslavia's production of oil tankers.[8] The shipyard is generally regarded as a model of efficient "self-managing socialism."

According to Segota's study, the 5,000-odd workers employed by the Third of May shipyard are divided into 672 self-management and sociopolitical units. These units hold 11,525 meetings a year for a total of 31,911 hours. Thus, Segota calculates, each worker at the shipyard spends 26.8 eight-hour working days a year at meetings! Translated into production, this is equivalent to one small tanker a year. Needless to say, Segota stresses that the meetings are essential to preserve the self-managing society.

The trend is the same in every industry in Yugoslavia. No one, to date, has dared to calculate the staggering loss to the country's hard-pressed economy. If anything, the tendency has been to increase rather than decrease the rhythm of the meetings. In this sense, the official Yugoslav version that "self-management is no longer an experiment, it has taken root" is quite true. The workers clearly prefer to discuss rather than work, particularly if this does not affect their pay. Short of drastic surgery or the disintegration of Titoism, self-management would, indeed, be hard to uproot. Periodic calls for an increase in productivity have yet to be felt.

Tito himself has wondered in a number of speeches why Yugoslav workers in West Germany or Sweden perform so much better than their counterparts at home. The answer, it seems, is obvious enough. Their foreign employers can afford to pay higher wages, not being shackled by the waste of self-management.

Apart from the intricate and often bewildering maze of workers' councils and their various offshoots, the main difference between the Yugoslav and orthodox communist systems is the fact that while in the Soviet Union and the satellite countries the system is totally centralized, the Yugoslav planning doctrine does not attempt to allocate physical resources.

Few prices are government-dictated; most fluctuate according to the market economy. The five-year-plan system mainly establishes the framework under which the economy operates. Officially, there is no attempt at detailed control. But the party does oversee the economy, does discipline workers and managers, and does make sure that priorities fit with its overall objectives. Consequently, the party is the ultimate arbiter, and loyalty to the party and to Titoism more often than not is more important than professional performance.

A word should be mentioned about the question of strikes. In a purely communist country, any work stoppage is illegal. The theory behind it is that "workers cannot strike against themselves." The Yugoslavs have never solved this ticklish problem, although the inclination seems to be against tolerating strikes. The result is typical of the entire tenor of the system: strikes are neither allowed nor forbidden. The government deals with them strictly on an ad hoc basis.

According to Neca Jovanov, a trade union official, some 2,000 strikes took place in Yugoslavia in the 11-year period between 1958 and 1969.[9] (Jovanov has no figures for the more recent years.) By Western standards, the number is minimal; by Communist standards, simply staggering. On the one hand, it proves a certain liberty of action enjoyed by Yugoslav workers; on the other, it tends to show the degree of imperfection of self-management, which has forced the "managers" themselves to use such a drastic weapon by Marxist standards.

Jovanov argues that Yugoslav strikes have been the result of "disharmony between the real and the imaginary status of the working class." He further points out the existence of a serious conflict between blue-collar and white-collar workers and says:

> Striking workers' earnings are calculated on the basis of assessments of their work made by the people against whom they are striking; the latter receive their salaries (and other remuneration) on the basis of their function—primarily the managerial level on which they operate.

Jovanov admits that in such circumstances, it would be difficult to describe the system as real "workers' self-management." What his study points out—without saying so—is that a simmering conflict sets the Yugoslav workers against the technocrats, who, not untypically, have loomed as "exploiters."

The Yugoslav party cadres are divided on the issue of strikes. Tito himself on occasion has suggested strikes as a "just weapon." Mika Spiljak, president of the Trade Union Confederation, warned in May 1976 that union leaders should not react to strikes "in a nervous or affronted manner; it would be even worse for them to try to find the culprits or organizers of the strikes." The real culprits, according to Spiljak, "are the leaders . . . who have brought about such a situation in enterprises and failed to take the necessary measures to involve the entire working collective in the search for a solution."[10]

There are a number of economists in Yugoslavia who deplore the country's rush toward a factory-type civilization. They point out that with the proper accent on its agricultural potential, Yugoslavia could become the breadbasket of Europe. Instead, it is forced to import some food products. But in any Communist state, factories mean progress, the fulfillment of the dream of the backward and underdeveloped. The price does not seem to matter—until much later.

The self-management concept, as practiced at this stage, consists basically of three major components: workers' councils in industry, self-managing bodies in schools and other social institutions, and self-management at the level of the commune, the basic administrative unit. Denitch thus described the different approaches to self-management:

> Managers and technical experts stress plant and enterprise autonomy and their right to manage without interference of the government or central economic bodies. Politically conscious workers interpret self-management as their right to control the managerial staffs and to make the significant day-to-day decisions affecting their lives. Socialist intellectuals regard self-management as an alternative to a highly structured, party-dominated political system, and one that will create new norms and therefore hopefully a new socialist man. . . .
>
> Self-management in Yugoslavia represents an experiment of sufficient duration for it to begin to answer some of the basic questions. . . .

And Denitch concludes, "The experiment was successful since, even under conditions that were far from optimal, a working system of self-management developed, producing a dynamic economy and a degree of participation hitherto unknown in industrial society."[11]

This view surprises even some Yugoslav officials, few of whom in conversation with foreign guests speak of self-management in such superlative terms. On the contrary, in the past few years the accent has been on the failures rather than the accomplishments of the system.

The economic performance, which slumped badly in the first half of 1975 because of recession in the West, picked up considerably in the latter part of the year and in the first six months of 1976. On the whole, a 5.6 percent rate of growth is predicted for 1976. Inflation, which at one point reached 30 percent, is expected to drop to 11 percent by the end of 1976, which is roughly the West European level.

There remain a host of problems for which the government has no immediate remedy. Low productivity is one of them. The fact that Yugoslav prices are still too high by world standards reduces the competitiveness of Yugoslav goods (which in any case are considered below Western quality). The need to create more jobs is still great and leads to permanent conflict between economists and party cadres. In the cases where jobs have been artifically created for the sake of political expediency, efficiency dropped considerably. And there are no signs on the horizon that all these crucial problems will ease when Tito's successors take over.

Quite a few Yugoslav economists believe it would be in the country's interest to expand its trade with the Eastern bloc's Comecon rather than with the West. Compared to Eastern products, Yugoslav goods are of higher quality, and there is a constant demand for them. Indeed, in the first few months of 1976, Yugoslavia extended trade agreements with all East European Comecon countries for the next five years. These agreements reflect the trend of the steady growth of economic exchanges between Yugoslavia and the Soviet bloc: its volume is expected to more than double by 1980 to nearly $29 billion. All indications are that sooner or later, Comecon will become Yugoslavia's most important trading partner. The figures for the past two years are outspoken enough: while in 1975, Yugoslav trade with the Soviet bloc, including the Soviet Union, represented 29.5 percent of the total, the percentage in the first nine months of 1976 grew to 35. While attractive from the point of view of sales of Yugoslav goods, this trend worries many Yugoslav planners. The growing trade involvement with the Soviet bloc is not seen as a happy omen. It may one day seriously limit Yugoslavia's political choices.

There has been a considerable growth of Western investment in the country, currently surpassing $1 billion. The present five-year economic development plan calls for an annual foreign investment increase of 8.5 percent, including loan and credit financing. Dow Chemical is building a major petrochemical complex worth $750 million. The Westinghouse Corporation will participate in the building of Yugoslavia's first nuclear power plant in a joint venture with the republics of Slovenia and Croatia, the most advanced in the Yugoslav federation. Important as these projects are, they generate few jobs. It is significant that a number of Western companies prefer to wait before plunging capital into Yugoslavia until a clear political pattern in connection with Tito's succession emerges.

The Yugoslav government, on the whole, feels that the strength of the country's economy will be crucial in guaranteeing its survival and the success of its foreign policy. A country which is politically and economically shaky can hardly expect to carry much weight on the international scene. In the words of a typical technocrat, Mladen Soic, who promotes Western investment in the country, "The strength of Yugoslavia's international impact is based on economic progress." There has, indeed, been considerable progress, particularly if one remembers the depth of disaster into which the country was plunged as a result of World War II. But at the same time, the policy of open frontiers has led to a free movement of Yugoslav labor west and has created high expectations. So far, the regime has not been able to satisfy these expectations. The inhabitants of such republics as Croatia and Slovenia particularly feel their standard of living could have been considerably higher without forced contributions to the other republics. It is a dangerous feeling, likely to be given more impetus in the years to come. The concept of self-management may have been firmly implanted, and the republics, to a certain extent, have been made economically interdependent. Yet there are no guarantees that the system will be able to withstand the post-Tito difficulties. Considering the overall philosophical orientation of the Yugoslav Communist movement, the steady growth of trade with the Soviet bloc, the Soviet Unions's interest in the Balkans, and warnings about the need to look at the economy more "in Marx's sense," one can hardly be optimistic about Yugoslavia's economic future.

NOTES

1. *Borba*, May 28, 1976.
2. Djilas, op. cit., pp. 104, 67-68.
3. *Vjesnik*, February 1, 1976.
4. *Borba,* September 19, 1975.
5. *Politika*, November 10, 1975.
6. *Gledista*, no 3, Belgrade, March 1970.
7. Bogdan Denitch, *The Legitimation of a Revolution: The Yugoslav Case* (New Haven: Yale, 1976), p. 10.
8. Ivan Segota. Privately circulated.
9. Neca Jovanov, "Workers' Strikes in the Socialist Federative Republic of Yugoslavia between 1958 and 1969," cited in *Vecernje Movosti*, May 15, 1976.
10. *Vecernje Novosti*, May 15, 1976.
11. Denitch, op. cit., pp. 175, 182.

CHAPTER

7

AGAINST ALL POINTS OF THE COMPASS

> The task of our army is not merely to defend the territorial integrity of our country, but also to defend our socialism when we see that it is in danger and that it cannot be defended by other means.
>
> Josip Broz Tito,
> December 22, 1971

When Soviet armor rolled into Czechoslovakia in August, 1968, Yugoslavia's concept of European security was all but shattered. The Yugoslav army was deployed mainly in the coastal areas, in anticipation of another Middle Eastern crisis.* Tito himself, as was noted previously, had publicly insisted he did not believe that the Soviets would intervene in Czechoslovakia.[1] Needless to say, the events of that August had a sobering effect on the country's leadership. The whole defense concept was hurriedly revised, leading to the creation of what is known as General People's Defense. This, in turn, led to the enactment of the National Defense Law of 1969, spelling out the organization and a complicated chain of command.

The aim is to turn the country into a bastion capable of resisting any foreign invader until outside factors begin to intervene in Yugoslavia's favor. This, basically, is the degree of Yugoslav military leverage: regardless of how successful or unsuccessful the country is in opposing an invading force, external factors must intervene. Without them, the country can offer stubborn but

*Some diplomatic reports from Belgrade speculated about a rumor that following the 1967 Arab-Israeli war, the Yugoslav defense forces were integrated for a time into Soviet contingency planning in the event of a more generalized conflict in the area.

basically pointless resistance—assuming that the invading force belongs to a nation or bloc larger and stronger than Yugoslavia.

In keeping with its policy of nonalignment, Yugoslavia has not done much to create any residue of goodwill in any of the powers that might come to its assistance. It is simply assumed that the Warsaw Pact would not tolerate any Western encroachment on Yugoslav territory, while NATO would take a dim view of any direct Soviet threat against what is generally considered its outer perimeter. The view is based more on hope than on hard facts and rests on fragile foundations—as does the entire defense concept in a multinational state which has yet to feel itself one nation.

But while the various republics have frequently shown a tendency to foster their own interests rather than those of the federation, the YPA has on the whole become a reasonably welded, all-Yugoslav organization. Increasingly, it is regarded as the ultimate guardian not only of Yugoslavia's territorial integrity but of its political doctrine as well. The army's efficiency is heightened by the fact that it is the only organization in Yugoslavia not shackled by the constraints of self-management. This, as will be explained later, is not the case with the Territorial Defense Force (TDF), which is organized along regional and thus nationalist lines. Although the TDF is an admirable concept on paper and to some extent has been patterned on the Swiss and Swedish systems, its eventual success in Yugoslav conditions remains debatable.

Despite the strong accent on popular defense, the regular army, or more specifically the YPA's career officer corps, remains an all-important political element. It is regarded by many foreign observers as the ultimate arbiter on the political scene. The tendency has been clear: a senior army officer, General Franjo Herljević, is minister of internal affairs, controlling both branches of the all-pervasive security system. Kontraobabestajna Sluzba (KOS), the military intelligence, has emerged as the main prop of the security apparatus. Together with the civilian security police, Sluzba Državne Bezbednosti (SDB), it has been keeping Yugoslavia together.* It is increasingly felt that in the event of post-Tito difficulties, the YPA, in close collaboration with the party, will be the main force capable of preventing the federation's falling apart. Assuming that, short of a major crisis, the Soviet Union has no intention of intervening militarily, the army's role will be to make sure that the country does not give in to the combination of internal pressures threatening it.

The prevailing view is that if the army holds together, there is no reason to believe that the Yugoslav federation cannot hold together. In this respect, the army will have the full-fledged backing of the LCY simply because the party can only survive as a unit if Yugoslavia survives. That much has been spelled out by Tito himself.

---

*In references to the Yugoslav security apparatus, its old name, Uprava Državne Bezbednosti (UDBA), is frequently applied.

On the basis of this premise, some analysts firmly believe in the inevitability, if not of a military takeover after Tito, at least of strong military interference in the state apparatus. That interference may be of limited duration, but any such possibility has to be viewed with extreme caution: generally, when a military caste develops a taste for power, it is highly difficult to persuade it to relinquish that power. As it is, the degree of military participation in Yugoslavia's political life is greater than that in any other socialist country, perhaps with the exception of East Germany. To wit: In 1974 there were 21 senior army officers elected to the party's Central Committee. At this writing, they have a major voice in virtually all fields of state activity. The military is involved in political decision making at the highest level. The process, consequently, has in effect begun. It remains to be seen whether it survives the test of time and the strains of the post-Tito transition. One thing is certain: As time goes by and doubts emerge as to the country's future course, the army will increasingly begin to regard itself as the guarantor of Yugoslav unity. It should be pointed out, however, that the reason military dictatorships have not existed in Communist countries is that any Communist army is a party army, more often than not treated as the party's own weapon. This also is the case in Yugoslavia. Such an interlocking relationship does not preclude an increased role for the military in the party and state apparatus, without the stigma of military takeover.

To understand the nature of the Yugoslav military establishment, a glance backward is essential. The Yugoslav army's tradition is based almost exclusively on the fierce partisan struggle of World War II. Any prewar tradition has faded away–along with the Serb generals who believed in God and Greater Serbia, the mustachioed Russian advisers who sought shelter in Yugoslavia after the defeat of the White armies by the Bolsheviks, and the roar "May God help you" which thundered along ramrod-straight ranks inspected by bemedaled officers. That vision came to a crashing end during the ten-day German-Italian blitz in April 1941, compared with which the earlier German advances against Poland and France seemed unbelievably slow. The Serb-dominated Yugoslav military establishment, with its antiquated R-41 mobilization plan calling for the fielding of 28 infantry and three cavalry divisions, was later blamed for the nation's swift collapse. The subsequent procrastination of General Draža Mikhailović's "chetniks" most of whom were former regular soldiers, did little to help the prewar army's prestige.* The chetniks were more preoccupied with fighting the Communists than the Germans and in the latter stages of the war collaborated with the Axis armies. The new, rugged forces of Tito's partisans, led by men

---

*The word "chetnik" stems from the Serbian word "četa," or "military company." The chetnik movement was Serb in its orientation rather than all-Yugoslav. In the end, despite considerable help by the Western Allies, it became fragmented and torn by internal feuds. Mikhailović himself was captured, and executed after a month-long trial in 1946.

steeped in the principles of Marxism and looking with admiration to the Soviet model, bore the brunt of World War II resistance.

The initial postwar years saw the emergence of a comparatively large regular army based on the Soviet pattern. There was little room for improvisation, and Soviet advisers tended to scoff at the partisan tradition. It was only after the break with the Cominform in 1948 that the Yugoslav army attempted to create its own specific image and doctrine.

As the threat of Soviet military intervention diminished in the 1950s, so did the military budget. Thus, while in 1952 the Yugoslav state spent $678 million on the military, or 19.2 percent of its net material product (a socialist term for total product), the amount dropped to $475 million, or 9.8 percent of NMP by 1956. At the time of the Czech invasion in 1968, the budget stood at $614 million, or 5.7 percent of NMP.

In the period immediately preceding the invasion of Czechoslovakia, there was little concern among the Yugoslav leaders about Soviet intentions. Quite to the contrary, Tito and his aides were warning about the threat posed by "Western imperialism." The Yugoslav military establishment conducted war games oriented toward defense against a NATO attack, while the Yugoslav press was writing about the U.S. conduct in Vietnam and the possibility of another Middle East crisis. Tito himself was concerned about "the posture of imperialism" in the Middle East as a result of the 1967 Arab-Israeli war and in other areas in the aftermath of the ousters of Sukarno in Indonesia, Nkrumah in Ghana, and Ben Bella in Algeria. Tito's "progressive" friends were losing not only ground but their thrones and palaces as well, and the Old Partisan saw it as part of an imperialist conspiracy. The marshal was accusing "Western imperialism" of undermining peace in Europe, Africa, and Asia. He showed no obvious alarm at the roar of Soviet, Polish, Hungarian, and East German armor maneuvering on Czechoslovakia's borders.

Yugoslavia thus misread the political situation in a surprisingly inept manner. In a democratic country, the postmortems would have been bitter and probably would have resulted in a change of leadership. In Yugoslavia, the only known victim of the faulty strategic planning was General Ivan Gosnyak, at the time deputy supreme commander of the armed forces. He was stripped of his military and party role, apparently for having left undefended the crucial Hungarian and Bulgarian borders—the main possible points of Soviet entry into Yugoslavia. Whether Gosnyak alone was responsible for keeping two thirds of Yugoslavia's forces in Croatia and the coastal areas has not been explained.

Ultimately, the government's reaction indicated considerable alarm. To the Belgrade inner sanctum, the Soviet Union once again loomed as the major potential enemy. Hurriedly, officers in the gray uniforms of the People's Army, gold stars glistening on their shoulder boards, began drawing plans that would make Soviet invaders pay a steep price for attacking Yugoslavia. And in this the country seemed unanimous: Yugoslavia was not Czechoslovakia; there would be no walkover.

The new military concept of creating a vast defense apparatus that would involve most able-bodied men and quite a few women had been under discussion for some time. The country, it was felt, should face the enemy unified, without differences between armed citizens and a military caste. The view was expressed in these words by the Defense Minister General Ljubičić'

> There is not a hierarchy of elements in the system of nation-wide defence, but a combination of reactions in which any success by one expands the radius for action by others; partial failures are therefore easier to bear and their negative consequences may be more rapidly eliminated.[2]

The big problem was to translate the views of this indisputable strategist into reality insofar as the organization of Yugoslavia's armed forces was concerned. Yet the discussion went on with the accent on World War II partisan successes. The doctrine, as it emerged by the middle of 1968, was best described by Major General Mirko Vranic.[3] According to him, the classical units of the regular army as well as the territorial units would wage war, oscillating between frontal attacks and guerrilla action. He proposed equipping the territorial units with tanks and making the territorial interchangeable with regular units by relegating the bulk of the well-trained army reservists to the TDF.

Before the concept's final elaboration in the National Defense Law of 1969, serious political factors had to be considered. The Yugoslav military has always looked up to the Soviet model, and no amount of hostility toward the Soviet Union could change that. For many generals, the West has remained the traditional potential enemy, regardless of what happened in Hungary in 1956 or Prague in 1968. Few men who led partisan units, with the Red Star on their forage caps and Communist literature in their rucksacks, were likely to be converted into ardent believers in Western democracy.

The sizable U.S. military aid to Yugoslavia ($700 million from 1951 to 1959) has not led to increased contact between the Yugoslav and American military establishments. It has not created any bonds. The Yugoslav military has remained distrustful of the West and particularly of the United States. Because of the very nature of any military organization, the army has an inherent interest in a strong, centralized government. Above all, the Yugoslav generals are concerned with keeping their forces well armed. In 1976 the bulk of imported sophisticated equipment, such as missiles, came from the Soviet Union. As stated earlier, contacts between high-ranking officers of the two countries were becoming more and more frequent. While no one questions the patriotism of the Yugoslav military leaders, it can be concluded that within the present geopolitical context, they have more at stake in a working relationship with the Soviet Union than with the West.

But nonalignment has had an impact on the military as well. Consequently, the doctrine of popular defense included the inevitable principle of the defense against "all points of the compass." But while Charles de Gaulle, with his vision of French grandeur and military possibilities, could conceivably indulge in such schemes, the very idea that a Balkan country of 20 million could adopt a similar doctrine raises eyebrows. But in the end, the idea prevailed: in the eyes of Yugoslav military planners, both superpowers had become potential enemies. Prague illustrated Soviet intentions; Vietnam, U.S. ones.

In keeping with the need to provide for every possible military contingency, for nationalist claims, and for the intricate political and administrative system, the defense law runs fully 183 articles. The preamble states that

> Socialist Yugoslavia is making preparations for general people's defence in case it is attacked and its freedom, independence, sovereignty and territorial integrity are jeopardized; it is determined to oppose any possible aggressor with all its forces and means. . . .
>
> Taking as a point of departure the socialist, self-managing and democratic character of the Yugoslav community of equal nations and nationalities, and the nature of modern war as an all-embracing armed conflict in which boundary lines between the front and the rear, and between the people and the army, disappear, Socialist Yugoslavia, utilizing the experience of the People's Liberation War, is developing its own conception of general people's defence as the only possible form of opposing armed aggression.[4]

The defense plan is simple enough: the regular army, bolstered by reservists to the strength of some half a million men, fights a rearguard action long enough to allow the rest of the country to mobilize an estimated 3 million men, backed by 1.3 million civil defense workers. Subsequently, every commune, every town, every major factory, becomes a "hedgehog" that will eventually roll up an invading force of some 2 million men, or roughly 8 soldiers per square kilometer.

In the wake of the adoption of this concept, the country's defense forces underwent a profound reorganization. In 1976, the regular army, which serves as the training force for reservists, consisted of some 190,000 men. The air force had 20,000 and the navy about 19,000. While in peacetime the TDF consists of only 3,000 instructors, this force can (theoretically) be expanded to 1.5 million men within 48 hours. The eventual target is 3 million men in territorial defense units. With the regular army and civil defense workers, this would represent an impressive number of some 5 million men, or 25 percent of the population.

The concept of mass mobilization is the first obvious flaw in the Yugoslav defense plan. It is questionable how long a nation under attack can survive if most of its able-bodied men and women are engaged in defensive tasks, thus paralyzing industry, transportation networks, administration, and other equally important fields essential to a country's survival. Israeli strategiests, relying on the lightninglike mobilization of an estimated 10 percent of the country's population, have never resolved the problem satisfactorily, The 1973 war with the Arabs, which required maintaining under the colors some 300,000 men for at least three months, dramatically underlined the impact of such a mass conscription on industry. And yet Israel was not really invaded: it merely defended a perimeter well outside its own frontiers and subsequently kept watch against the possibility of another enemy thrust. The Yugoslav defense doctrine assumes a direct attack by airborne and armored troops from several directions.

The second flaw is in the distribution of the population. The former partisans who drafted the doctrine used their World War II resistance as a model and inspiration. The Yugoslavia they have helped to create no longer consists of scattered and inaccessible mountain villages. Vast industrial complexes—notoriously easy targets—have been created. The urban population has grown by 20 percent since the end of the war—to the detriment of the rural population that would provide the proverbial "water" for the guerrilla "fish." World War II resistance against the Axis forces flourished in the countryside but was limited in the cities. Now the task before the Yugoslav military is to defend what has basically become an industrial country. The 2,000 or so factories in which self-defense units have been organized may well form defensive "hedgehogs," but their vulnerability in the face of air and ground attacks cannot be denied. Urban society could hardly become a successful guerrilla bastion. At best, well-defended cities can tie up sizable enemy units without having direct impact on the conduct of war, as the ill-fated Warsaw uprising of 1944 sufficiently demonstrated. The 40,000-odd fighters were basically trapped in a city of 1 million inhabitants, mercilessly pounded by the enemy from the sky and on the ground.

The third flaw in the system stems from Yugoslavia's complicated national setup. According to Adam Roberts of the London School of Economics, the authority given to the different component republics over the territorial defense system has created "not a nation in arms, but nations in arms."[5] The requirements of instant mobilization and defense of an immediate area have turned the TDF into a very much locally oriented force. To wit: In the event of attack, the Montenegrins will defend objectives in their area, while the Croats will fight in their own territory. Since the TDF will comprise the bulk of Yugoslavia's fighting men, what would be easier in the event of political difficulties than a split along national lines? In effect, the fully mobilized TDF would give the two major republics, Serbia and Croatia, reasonably large armies.

History is full of examples of such "citizens' armies" weighing heavily on the conduct of war and in some cases paralyzing it. The Siege of Paris in 1870-71 by the Prussians is a classic example. There, the commanding French generals were more concerned about the attitude of the 300,000 national guardsmen than about other purely military considerations.

The defense law itself supplies the fourth flaw in the system—and a serious one at that. Under it, the army is not in sole charge of organizing defense. The republics, autonomous regions, and communes are to play an equally important role. The division of responsibilities was spelled out in the following manner:

the central government in Belgrade is responsible for arming and preparing the regular army for the defense of Yugoslavia. But units of the TDF—thus, the bulk of Yugoslavia's fighting men—"are established by the commune, province and republic." Even in wartime, local civilian authorities are to "direct the general people's resistance on their territory."[6]

In addition to the political implications of such a system, it is not too difficult to imagine the chaos in the chain of command in wartime conditions. The best-organized armies frequently stumble over such problems as who has responsibility over a given sector. With fronts collapsing in a war of movement, the vision of commune self-management councils haggling with regular army generals over logistic and other problems is terrifying indeed.

The defense law ordered that each commune, province, and republic create its own national defense staffs—an additional burden on Yugoslav workers already spending 20 percent of their working time on self-management. The law specifies the need to coordinate defense planning within the republics and with the regular army. In the event of the presence of an army unit in the territory of a given commune, "the territorial defense units are subordinated to the command of the YPA unit with which they co-operate in the execution of their common combat task."[7] Yet, in areas overrun by the enemy, the role of directing defense falls to the defense staff of the given republic.

The same division exists at a higher level. Thus, the law specifies that while the supreme command of the armed forces is in charge of the operational (regular) army, "the republic national defence staffs are in charge of territorial defence."[8] This blueprint for commanding "nations in arms" was somewhat modified in the subsequent defense law of 1974 by the following phrase: "The supreme direction and command of the armed forces ensures the unity and inseparability of the armed forces and the armed struggle. The President of the Republic is the Supreme Commander of the armed forces."[9] The new law, while not drastically different from the previous one, makes a provision for united commands for the TDF and the YPA.

It is not the purpose of this study to discuss in detail the workings of the Yugoslav military and territorial defense. Yet their organization and possibilities are vital to the survival of Yugoslavia as an entity. An analysis of the often confusing directives, laws, and spheres of responsibility does not, on the whole, offer an encouraging picture. The concept of General People's Defense in itself is the best the country could come up with within the context of its ideological position. Unfortunately, the nature of Yugoslavia's national and administrative organization might make the plan difficult to put into effect. And the fact that nearly 1 million able-bodied Yugoslavs are at any time employed in the West is a direct threat to any mobilization plans. Tito himself has said that the workers in the West represent the equivalent of three large armies.

Ever since the Soviet invasion of Czechoslovakia, constant maneuvers have been conducted in Yugoslavia with the accent on territorial defense. Up to 1 million men and women have been called up for such exercises, as usual aimed against "all points of the compass." Laconic government communiqués shed little light on the smoothness and performance of the TDF. Western military attachés are faced with Yugoslav suspicions and can only obtain scanty information. It is thus difficult to evaluate the preparedness of the TDF.

Of some importance may be the counterproductive impact of intensive Communist propaganda, which is an inseparable part of the indoctrination of the TDF. By now, young people in Yugoslavia resent being subjected to the same, frequently stale slogans. The policy of open frontiers has made travel west within the reach of the average Yugoslav. While willing to take an active part in defense preparations, the young generation is becoming hostile to the propaganda that goes with it. The partisan aura has paled. The stout, middle-aged veterans with their stories of World War II exploits no longer amuse or inspire many young people.

It is generally assumed that the new Yugoslav man will have the same combat spirit as his father or grandfather had during the fierce partisan resistance. New political and social concepts, however, have radically transformed Yugoslav society. It was one thing to resist the Axis powers, knowing that a powerful combination of allies was on Yugoslavia's side. A swift, airborne-armored invasion of Yugoslavia today might not arouse the same response and determination.

These possible negative factors aside, it should be stressed that Yugoslavia has done as much as it can under difficult circumstances to prepare for military confrontation in specific conditions. The accent, in the regular army as in the territorial defense, is on antitank and antiaircraft weapons. Armor is not believed vitally essential: tanks are expensive, and their ability to maneuver in mountain terrain is questionable.* Although General Vranic did suggest equipping the territorial units with tanks, he apparently meant mainly light armored vehicles and these not in large numbers. Military aircraft of Yugoslav construction are exceptionally light and capable of taking off and landing on short, grass airstrips. Their production, however, has been limited. In the fall of 1976, plans for the joint construction with Romania of a Yugoslav-designed fighter plane appeared to have bogged down. There is a strong accent on helicopters to assure the mobility of the defense forces. The navy has concentrated on the construction of small, comparatively cheap craft, such as patrol vessels, torpedo boats, minesweepers, and some submarines. Even the Yugoslav assault rifle of recent manufacture is much lighter than its predecessor. The infantryman's equipment has been reduced to the barest minimum.

There has been periodic speculation in the Western media about Yugoslavia's ability to construct its own atomic weapons, at least of the tactical

---

*Yugoslav armor consists of a disparate assembly of Soviet tanks as well as vintage American Shermans.

variety. The speculation was heightened after a visit by Defense Minister General Ljubičić to the atomic plant at Vinca. The visit prompted the military commentator of Belgrade's *Borba* to write, "A Yugoslav bomb will be built. In case of the danger of nuclear war, our land will be able to defend itself. . . . The production of cheaper and lighter atomic weapons which can hold back an aggressor is available. . . ."[10] There was little further comment on this somewhat surprising statement. At this stage, however, Western military observers are skeptical about Yugoslavia's nuclear capability. The Yugoslav government has signed the nuclear nonproliferation treaty.

The 1974 constitution clearly states that it is the duty of every citizen to defend his country. Moreover, Article 238 specifies that "no one shall have the right to acknowledge or sign an act of capitulation nor to accept or recognize the occupation of the Federal Socialist Republic of Yugoslavia or of any of its individual parts."

As mentioned earlier, the defense concept is to hold out as long as possible until outside factors can intervene. Roberts compared the defense plan to "a detonator. Whether or not it could actually defeat an enemy, it could create unpredictable reverberations. . . ."[11]

And the scale of such reverberations could be enormous indeed. No one—in Yugoslavia, in the East, or in the West—underestimates it. This in a way has created a feeling that nothing radical is likely to happen in Yugoslavia. It is a convenient theory, but it is better for all concerned if its validity is not tested.

While the creation of the territorial defense system based on regional units and regional command may prove dangerous to Yugoslavia's unity, much has been done to make the regular army an all-Yugoslav fighting instrument. The pre-World War II Yugoslav army was entirely dominated by Serbs, who, along with the Montenegrins, had developed a considerable military tradition. While today, Serbia (with a population ratio of 39.7 percent) still provides 60 percent of all officers and Croatia (with 23 percent of the population) supplies only 14 percent of the officers, the high command structure shows a much more even national balance. According to Roberts, "of the 24 highest military commanders in 1971, only 33 percent were Serbs, while 38 percent were Croats."[12]

Assuming that in the first years of the post-Tito era the army's main task will be to keep Yugoslavia together rather than repel an outside attack, this is a factor of major importance. To reiterate an earlier assessment: If the high command is determined enough and exercises enough control over the YPA, Yugoslavia has a strong chance of remaining one nation. The nature of its regime and the degree of its cooperation with Moscow depend on a host of factors that will emerge only when Tito is no longer on the scene.

The immediate task of the regular army after Tito's death will be extremely delicate. On the one hand, it will have to deploy its forces at the most vulnerable points of the frontiers, simply as a matter of precaution. The army will have to be on hand to protect the 700,000 Serbs in Croatia, who might easily be the first victims of resurgent Croat nationalism. The army has to be present in the autonomous region of Kosovo because of the tension between its Albanian and Serb inhabitants. Furthermore, the army must be in reasonable strength and readiness in Macedonia because Macedonia's immediate neighbor, Bulgaria, has not given up its claims to the area. Bulgaria is also the Soviet Union's staunchest and virtually unconditional ally in the Balkans and a possible invasion route from the south.

It is no small task for a comparatively small regular army. And should nationalist tensions begin to rock Yugoslavia's foundation, recourse to partial mobilization might be necessary. Given the nature and composition of the territorial defense, this might become a double-edged sword.

When nationalist student riots swept Zagreb, the capital of Croatia, in December of 1971, Tito seriously considered using the army. Fortunately for him and Yugoslavia, there was no need for such a drastic step. The army's presence was generally demonstrated by helicopter overflights and a state of alert. But it was an indication that Tito was willing to go far to preserve the country's unity. His successors might be tempted by a similar stratagem. Whether or not the army command follows them will depend on the degree to which the army is associated with the running of the state. And here, all indications are that the army is moving to become an important arbiter in post-Tito Yugoslavia.

The picture of the Yugoslav military machine would not be complete without a further word about the security apparatus. As mentioned earlier, it consists of the military security, KOS, and the civilian SDB (often called UDBA), both under the command of General Herljević. Both have been undergoing considerable reorganization, parallel with the political tightening up during the last years of Tito's rule.

In this study of Yugoslav-Soviet relations made for London's Institute for the Study of Conflict, Stephen Clissold advances the following view:

> Even while hunting down domestic Cominformists, UDBA, the Yugoslav security service, has preserved some links with the KGB and other Eastern European services and has continued to collaborate with them in such matters as trying to prevent citizens of those countries escaping to the West while holidaying in Yugoslavia. When Ranković, the powerful UDBA chief, was ousted in 1966 after his henchmen had been caught "bugging" Tito's own quarters, Brezhnev is reported to have intervened on his behalf, though Ranković had once been equally denounced along with Tito, Kardelj and the others as an anti-Soviet heretic. But UDBA remains a bastion of conservative Communist forces and an instrument for the repressive methods first learned from the Russians. That Tito and his heirs continue to rely on Soviet-style techniques to keep

> Soviet influences in check is likely to cause them not the least of their headaches.[13]

The author has been unable to find evidence of any strong links between the Yugoslav security forces and the Soviet Union's KGB. But then again, all research on the subject is seriously limited by the Yugoslav security laws. Knowledgeable diplomats in Belgrade, however, do not exclude the possibility of some form of cooperation between SDB and the Soviet intelligence network. They do agree that the security apparatus is committed to the idea of keeping Yugoslavia a Communist country.

The security apparatus in Yugoslavia is omnipresent and omnipotent. The country is believed to spend more money per capita on it than any other Communist state. The number of paid and unpaid informers (the latter tend to call themselves "social workers") is staggering. The workers abroad are thoroughly infiltrated, presumably to counter the influence of anti-Tito Yugoslav political émigrés. Student organizations are full of police informers. The reality of the SDB presence and knowledge is enough to prevent most Yugoslavs from openly criticizing the system.

The number of political arrests increased during 1975 and 1976. Western press dispatches from Yugoslavia have been reporting them conscientiously. In fact, to a cursory newspaper reader, Yugoslavia has been increasingly emerging as a country where most activity consists of jailing opponents of all sorts. According to Malcolm W. Browne, the resident correspondent for the New York *Times* in Belgrade:

> Yugoslavia may well have filled its jails with more political prisoners than any other country in Eastern Europe, except the Soviet Union. . . . The number held in Yugoslavia is not publicly known. The authorities said last year [1975] that 200 political prisoners had been added. A senior Communist official estimated that, since 1956, Yugoslav jails have held 8,000 political prisoners.[14]

This comment tends to bear out Clissold's assessment that Soviet-style methods are very much present in Yugoslavia. It should be mentioned, however, that political imprisonment is not the monopoly of Communist or Communist-oriented countries.

The after-Tito years are likely to witness continuing if not increasing cooperation between the military and the vast security apparatus. The two, under the overall supervision of the party, will thus emerge as guarantors of the Yugoslav system and the country's territorial integrity. If that happens, it will mean that the country will have to sacrifice a lot for the sake of staying united. Increasing military and security interference in government offers no guarantee, however, against Moscow's steady encroachment into Yugoslav affairs. It may keep the country together but it offers no guarantee of effective political independence of the kind Tito had in mind.

NOTES

1. *See* Chapter 4, p. 107.

2. A. Vuković et al., eds., "General People's Defense—The Guarantee of Independence for Socialist Yugoslavia," *The Yugoslav Concept of General People's Defence* (Belgrade: Medunarodna Politika, 1970), pp. 37-38; cited in Adam Roberts, *Nations in Arms: The Theory and Practice of Territorial Defence* (London: Chatto & Windus; New York: Praeger, 1976), pp. 173-74.

3. "The Strategic Employment of the Armed Forces in a General People's Defensive War," *The Yugoslav Concept of General People's Defense*, p. 252; cited in Roberts, op. cit., p. 176.

4. From the Introductory Principles of the National Defense Law, promulgated February 12, 1969; cited in Roberts, op. cit., p. 172.

5. Roberts, op, cit., p. 136.

6. From Articles 11, 14, 51, 52; ibid., p. 177.

7. From Article 26; cited in Roberts, op. cit., p. 178.

8. From Section III, Introductory Principles; cited in Roberts, op. cit., p. 179.

9. Cited in ibid.

10. December 7, 1975.

11. Roberts, op. cit., p. 194.

12. Ibid., p. 200.

13. Clissold, *Yugoslavia and the Soviet Union*, Conflict Studies, no. 57 (London: Institute for the Study of Conflict, 1975), p. 19.

14. New York *Times*, January 27, 1976.

CHAPTER

8

THE END OF AN ERA

> Nothing that has been created should be so sacred to us that it cannot be transcended and superseded by something still freer, more progressive and more human.
>
> Closing sentence of the program adopted by the League of Communists of Yugoslavia, Ljubljana, 1958

The scenario could be grim: Tito's successors are unable to impose their will on the feuding republics; nationalism, the historic bane of the Balkans, explodes with new strength, fueled by Kosovo's Albanian irredentism and the Croat clamor for more autonomy; the TDF, the pride of Yugoslavia's military planners, splits up along national lines; armed bands of Ustashi and Cominformist Soviet agents cross the borders, spreading terror and chaos.

Should that happen, further sequences are predictable: a violent political debate once again pits liberals against orthodox communists, the believers in more decentralization against the partisans of a strong federal government; the search for a viable solution is accompanied by a growing power struggle; one by one the republics proclaim their desire to have more control over their destiny; as the country cracks at the seams, the underground Cominformist party appeals to Moscow to save Yugoslavia from counterrevolution and disintegration. The Soviet Union has no choice but to respond positively to such a plea, assuring the West that it is acting only in the interest of world peace and détente. In any case, there is no need to fear Western reaction: after all, President Carter has said he would not send U.S. troops to fight in Yugoslavia.

But political predictions and scenarios are highly risky. It is more likely that no immediate dramatic changes will follow Tito's death. After all, the party and security apparatus are well entrenched and backed by the regular army. The tensions capable of splitting Yugoslavia have so far been contained—although no one knows for how long. What appears certain is that with Tito's death, one era of Yugoslavia's history will come to an end and a new one, fraught with danger, will begin.

Much depends on when the marshal decides to leave the political scene. It is quite conceivable that he will spend his last months or years in semiretirement, only symbolically presiding over Yugoslavia's destiny as the country's president-for-life. This, needless to say, would smooth the succession problems, although it would not reduce the obvious shock his death will cause. Tito has become a fixture in Yugoslav life, and particularly in recent years, his role as a symbol has been as important as his position as leader, international mediator, and domestic policy maker. Regardless of the frequent official claims that the post-Tito era has already begun, the impact of his death is bound to be enormous. On the other hand, it does not have to be destabilizing in its immediate consequences.

It is reasonably safe to assume that Tito's successors will make ringing pledges at his coffin to continue on the path he has mapped out. The party will maintain its grip according to the pattern established in the past few years. More likely than not, there will be a further political tightening up, as a preventive measure. The policy of free frontiers for Yugoslav citizens may be suspended for a time, or at least considerably limited.

How long relative calm is likely to last is difficult to estimate. Predictions range from six months to two years, although there are Yugoslavs and foreign analysts who do not exclude a much quicker pace of events, particularly if the Balkan Pandora's box is opened and a chain reaction—internal and external—sets in.

The author of this study is inclined to agree with the theory that, at least in the present international context, the possibility of a Soviet invasion can be excluded. This reasoning is based on the assumption that the Soviet leadership would stand to lose too much by such a rash expedition. The Soviets have labored hard to build up a reserve of goodwill in the West, including profitable trade and wheat shipments. The Soviet-dominated Warsaw Pact is faced with the serious problem of declining economic self-sufficiency. Many economists believe that the Soviet economy is becoming increasingly tied to commerce with the West. In 1976 alone, Soviet machinery and equipment imports from the West were expected to pass the $5-billion mark.[1] In addition to an obvious reluctance to destroy such essential and growing ties with the West, the Soviets do not really have to resort to a conspicuous and highly unpopular military operation to subjugate Yugoslavia. Time seems to be on Moscow's side in this respect. All the Soviets have to do is to stand by and watch the evolution of Yugoslavia's internal problems, at the same time activating all forces capable of playing into Soviet hands. These include the exploitation of possible dissatisfaction with Tito's successors, of nationalist rivalries and ambitions, and, above all, of the role of the underground Cominformist party.

Most students of the Yugoslav question generally assume that the Soviet Union will strive for a closer relationship with Yugoslavia—if not for overall control. According to Djilas, "Yugoslav Communism, as a form of national Communism, played an extremely important role in the weakening of Soviet imperialism. . . ."[2] Although in many cases the Yugoslav brand of nonalignment has converged with Soviet interests, Belgrade frequently has proved an embarrassment to the Soviet Union on the international scene. Above all, the Yugoslav system represents a possible attraction to the Soviet Union's East European satellites. Also, the Soviets want freer access to the Adriatic coast as part of their growing naval implantation in the Mediterranean. If one accepts the theory that the USSR's ultimate aim is to bring Yugoslavia back into the fold, or at least make it into a docile client-state, one should believe that the task is best accomplished with a minimum of shock. A slow, systematic subversion would be much more painless in all respects than a lighteninglike invasion.

The nature and extent of Soviet intervention depends to a great extent on the degree of national unity the post-Tito establishment manages to maintain. As mentioned earlier, the author believes that through firm cooperation between the party, the military, and the security apparatus, Yugoslavia's unity can be maintained for some time. But this solution in itself contains the germ of dissension if not revolt. No country kept together by force and repression is a happy country. It is merely a question of time before its unhappiness is translated into concrete action. The multinational makeup of Yugoslavia, its economic problems, and its open frontiers with the West are the kinds of factors which can easily propel the country into turmoil when the situation is ripe. If that happens, a different form of Soviet intervention might take place.

Not all factors capable of influencing the Yugoslav scene are negative, however. The interdependence of the republics, the comparative unity of the armed forces, and trade and tourism links with the West are among them. But perhaps the most important element is represented by the internal strains within the Communist camp and the possible repercussions throughout the world that an overt Soviet move in Yugoslavia might cause. The Soviet bloc is no longer the monolithic power it was twenty or even ten years ago. Increasing strains and stresses are emerging within the Soviet Union itself, and Moscow's relations with the satellite countries are slowly but constantly evolving. The West European Communist movement continues to regard Moscow with a considerable degree of political kinship, but the Soviet Union is no longer the uncontested ideological model.

The June 1976 East Berlin congress of Communist party chiefs was, in a way, a watershed. Although unwillingly, Moscow was forced to accept the view that all Communist parties have the right to choose their own "road to socialism" without interference by other members of the movement. The Soviet Union's acceptance of this principle, however, is believed to be mainly for external consumption. And it is not at all certain to what extent Brezhnev's successors will agree with it. Still, up to now the trend has been increasing rather than diminishing. As early as 1957, Djilas, the unquestionable authority on Yugoslavia's evolution, wrote that "the world center of Communist ideology no longer exists; it is in the process of complete disintegration. The unity of the world Communist movement is incurably injured."[3] With the benefit of hindsight, these were prophetic words. Further predictions along these lines, however, are risky.

There is a school of thought according to which the Soviet Union's ultimate aim in Yugoslavia is not necessarily to turn that country into an old-style obedient satellite. In the first place, this might be too difficult in the present situation; in the second, Yugoslavia may be much more useful as an outer-orbit satellite. In this role, Belgrade would still have its much-publicized policy of nonalignment, without the stigma of following Soviet instructions. Such aims are best served by a comparatively cautious policy which would tend to eliminate the use of armed might. Needless to say, the picture would change in the event of serious internal disturbances. In that case, an "invitation" either from one of the republics or the underground Communist party could be staged, and events would take a more dramatic turn.

Whatever happens, the West seems ill prepared and loath to react to any of these contingencies. For years, the muddle-through theory has been generally accepted, perhaps because the West finds wishful thinking easier than facing up to the possibility of a major turmoil in the Balkans. Yet Yugoslavia is important to the Western defense perimeter, and its subjugation would cause considerable dislocation of Western defenses. When mentioning the possibility of Soviet military involvement in Yugoslavia, one hears such stereotyped phrases as "NATO will not remain idle" and "the West will not tolerate Soviet military intervention in Europe." Yet, in 1977, one could hardly conceive of the United States as willing to plunge into another "brush-fire" war, even for the sake of keeping its perimeter intact. And NATO, basically, is the United States, as far as its willingness to act is concerned.

Direct or indirect military involvement in "limited" wars in different parts of the world has been practiced by most major powers since the end of World War II. But one does not contemplate easily a confrontation in the middle of the Balkans, so close to the heart of Europe. No one can guarantee that what sets out to be a limited war can be kept as such in the conditions of overwhelming Soviet "force de manoeuvre."

In the event that Yugoslavia ceases to be a neutral country, the question arises as to just what the impact on the West would be. The author believes that, although such a change would be serious and extremely uncomfortable, it would not represent an international disaster. There is no "domino theory" in Washington in the event of Yugoslavia's return into the Soviet orbit. The possibility is regarded as "grave" and "extremely serious" but not catastrophic. In short, the West could continue its rhythm of development and most of its foreign policy objectives regardless of whether Belgrade remains independent in the Titoist sense or reverts to membership in the Soviet Union's East European "alliance." The clock would merely be set back to 1948, with some serious readjustment of military planning in the Mediterranean.

True, Italy would become uneasy, extremely uneasy. Soviet pressure would intensify on Romania, probably resulting in that country's acknowledgment of Soviet hegemony. Albania might also follow suit after the death of Hoxha.

The by-products of the loss of Yugoslavia, however, might have a sobering effect on the attitude of the increasingly vocal Communist movements in such Western countries as Italy, France, and Spain. The relations between these movements and Moscow would be put under further strain. At the same time, a number of Western countries which have hitherto relegated the defense of NATO's perimeter to the United States might have second thoughts about military spending. France, most likely, would speed up its hitherto timid and slow process of reverting to increased cooperation with NATO. The differences between East and West, which tend to be glossed over by the concept of détente, would reemerge with all their implications. Yugoslavia's subjugation might not be a mere alarm bell. It could serve as a major rallying call, the cement that is needed for the wobbly Western community.

The author tends to agree with Western policy makers that continuation of the status quo in Yugoslavia would be the best solution. It seems unlikely, however, that Titoism can survive its founder in its present form. Too many internal and external factors are working against it.

It should be stressed that the West does have some leverage in the event of a Soviet military move against Yugoslavia. At one extreme of the spectrum, it can match Soviet force with its own force, including the nuclear deterrent. If the stakes are judged high enough, the West can engage in brinkmanship, regardless of the risks involved. The stakes, however, do not seem sufficiently high in the case of Yugoslavia. Unfortunately for Yugoslavia, the demise of Titoism can hardly be judged crucial to the West—provided the process is limited to Yugoslavia alone.

Where the West falls dramatically short of leverage possibilities is at the other, more likely end of the spectrum, a slow internal disintegration process the result of which would be Moscow's ultimate "peaceful" victory in Yugoslavia. And here, the fault would lie mainly with the Titoist system, which has for the sake of nonalignment consistently rejected any serious political rapprochement with the West. In a way, the Yugoslavs have boxed themselves into a dilemma: their anti-Western foreign policy has virtually ruled out U.S. and West European popular support for the cause of Yugoslav independence, although some such support exists among Western political leaders concerned about possible repercussions.

A dramatic change in Yugoslavia's foreign policy seems inconceivable, particularly during the last stages of Tito's rule. In the first place, such a change would undermine Yugoslavia's status in the Third World, one of the cornerstones of Titoism. At home, it would cause major ideological difficulties at a time when Yugoslavia needs as few problems as possible.

Other possible fields of Western influence in the post-Tito era are hampered by the fact that in contacts with Western diplomats and statesmen, the Yugoslavs have refused to discuss their problems with complete sincerity. Occasionally, they admit the existence of some potential difficulties. In most cases, however, they stick to the officially sanctioned line that Yugoslavia is one nation, Titoist and indivisible, and that the Soviet Union intends to honor its ideological "particularism." This virtually precludes any meaningful dialogue with the West centering on possible post-Tito contingency planning. Thus, any Western ability to help defuse or attenuate the problems looming ahead of Yugoslavia should be regarded as extremely limited. Whatever weak efforts existed have been rejected by the Yugoslavs themselves under the overall label of interference in a nonaligned country's internal affairs.

Some Western governments feel that potential leverage possibilities do exist in other fields. These include sales of Western arms to Yugoslavia to make it less dependent on the Soviet Union, at the same time increasing its defense capacity against invasion.* In the economic field, according to this view, the West can do a lot by increasing trade and Western participation in Yugoslav industry, assuming that the conditions are right. Finally, there is some room for more political contacts, including state visits, mutual declarations of friendship, and support for Yugoslav initiatives on the international scene. To what extent such demonstrations would help to reinforce Yugoslavia's position in the post-Tito era remains unclear. Also, it would be difficult for the West to give systematic backing to Yugoslavia's foreign policy proposals, since a great many of them are anti-Western in nature.

Consequently, it can be said that if Titoism dies one day, as is likely, it will be through its own doing. Deprived of the possibilities of influencing Yugoslavia's internal and external course, constantly attacked by Titoist diplomacy, the West will be reduced to the role of a silent and uneasy observer of Titoism's demise.

There is, of course, the Yugoslav theory that the two superpowers will automatically honor Yugoslav neutrality, even if only for their own sake. That theory may be valid as far as the West is concerned, but not necessarily for the Soviet Union. Treaties of the most formal character have been violated and rejected before when such an act suited one of the signatories. Besides, even assuming that both Moscow and Washington would pledge to stay out of

---

*Although the sale of U.S. arms was suspended *sine die* in 1976, negotiations continued with Britain and France, as well as limited shipments of such equipment as helicopters.

Yugoslavia, no such agreement would cover "peaceful" ways of influencing that nation's destiny. In any case, there were no signs in 1977 that the two superpowers were about to agree on a joint Yugoslav policy in a formal manner.

There remains one last theory: What if Yugoslavia after Tito turns Westward rather than Eastward? Here again, Titoism itself has virtually precluded such a possibility. Marxism as a concept is too deeply embedded where it really matters: in the ruling establishment, the army, and the security apparatus. The previously voiced hope that one day Yugoslavia would evolve toward a form of "democratic socialism" and thus "serve as a bridge between Social Democracy and Communism"[4] evaporated long ago. While many Yugoslavs would probably welcome such a radical change, they would hardly be in a position to foster it. Long years of Titoism seem to have condemned the country to espousing communism, even in a diluted form. A move toward a closer relationship with a Communist country is easier and more plausible than a move toward the West. Only a major international upheaval could change that. And no one, in the West or the East, really wants a cataclysm.

NOTES

1. From a report on the Soviet economy by the Joint Economic Committee of the U.S. Congress; quoted in the Washington *Post,* October 25, 1976.
2. Djilas, op. cit., p. 184.
3. Ibid., p. 183.
4. Ibid., p. 184.

SELECTED BIBLIOGRAPHY

Auty, Phyllis. *Tito: A Biography*. Rev. ed. Harmondsworth, England: Pelican, 1974.

Clissold, Stephen. *Yugoslavia and the Soviet Union*. Conflict Studies, no. 57. London: Institute for the Study of Conflict, 1975.

Denitch, Bogdan Denis. *The Legitimation of a Revolution: The Yugoslav Case*. New Haven: Yale, 1976.

Djilas, Milovan. *Conversations with Stalin*. New York: Harcourt, Brace & World, 1962.

———. *The New Class: An Analysis of the Communist System.* New York: Praeger, 1957.

Facts About Yugoslavia. Belgrade: Yugoslav Review, Federal Committee for Information, n.d.

Hoffman, George W., and Fred Warner Neal. *Yugoslavia and the New Communism.* New York: Twentieth Century Fund, 1962.

Johnson, A. Ross. *Yugoslavia: In the Twilight of Tito*. Washington Papers, vol. 2, no. 16. Beverly Hills: Sage Publications, Center for Strategic and International Studies, 1974.

Jovic, Borisav. *Economic Development of Yugoslavia*. Belgrade: Federal Committee for Information, 1975.

King, Robert R. "The Macedonian Question and Bulgaria's Relations with Yugoslavia." Mimeographed. Munich: Radio Free Europe, June 1975.

Pašić, Najdan. *The Socio-political System of Yugoslavia*. Translated by Bosko Milosavljevic. Belgrade: Federal Committee for Information, 1975.

Resolution on Joint Policy of the Economic and Social Development of Yugoslavia in 1976. Assembly Series, no. 261. Belgrade: Federal Committee for Information, Assembly of the Socialist Federal Republic of Yugoslavia, n.d.

Roberts, Adam. *Nations in Arms: The Theory and Practice of Territorial Defence*. Studies in International Security, no. 18. London: Chatto & Windus, International Institute for Strategic Studies: New York: Praeger, 1976.

Rusinow, Dennison I. *Crisis in Croatia*. 4 pts. Southeast Europe Series (Yugoslavia) 19, nos. 4-6. New York: American Universities Field Staff, 1972.

———. *A Note on Yugoslavia: 1972*. Southeast Europe Series (Yugoslavia) 19, no. 3. New York: American Universities Field Staff, 1972.

———. *Population Review 1970: Yugoslavia*. Southeast Europe Series (Yugoslavia) 17, no. 1. New York: American Universities Field Staff, 1970.

———. *Slovenia: Modernization Without Urbanization?* Southeast Europe Series (Yugoslavia) 20, no. 1. New York: American Universities Field Staff, 1973.

———. *Some Aspects of Migration and Urbanization in Yugoslavia*. Southeast Europe Series (Yugoslavia) 19, no 2. New York: American Universities Field Staff, 1972.

———. *The Yugoslav Concept of "All-National Defense."* Southeast Europe Series (Yugoslavia) 19, no. 1. New York: American Universities Field Staff, 1972.

———. *Yugoslavia's Return to Leninism*. Southeast Europe Series (Yugoslavia) 21, no. 1. New York: American Universities Field Staff, 1974.

PERIODICALS

Bertsch, Gary K. "Currents in Yugoslavia: The Revival of Nationalisms." *Problems of Communism*, November-December 1973, pp. 1-15.

Hammond, Thomas T. "Moscow and Communist Takeovers." *Problems of Communism*, January-February 1976, pp. 48-67.

Hoffman, George W. "Currents in Yugoslavia: Migration and Social Change." *Problems of Communism*, November-December 1973, pp. 16-31.

Hough, Jerry F. "The Brezhnev Era: The Man and the System." *Problems of Communism*, March-April 1976, pp. 1-17.

Yugoslav Survey 16, no. 4 (1975) and 17, no. 1 (1976), Belgrade.

INDEX

ABOUT THE AUTHOR

ANDREW BOROWIEC is a journalist who has written widely on international affairs. After 13 years as a foreign correspondent for the Associated Press, he joined the Washington *Star* in 1966 and for 10 years reported on Europe, the Middle East, and Africa. He is currently freelancing from his homes in Cyprus and France.

Mr. Borowiec received the 1963 Overseas Press Club award for "Best Reporting From Abroad," received a citation for same from the Overseas Press Club in 1965, and in 1971 he was given the Washington-Baltimore Guild Front Page Award for international reporting. The author holds an M.S. from the Columbia School of Journalism.